"*flourish* is a rig  creative person. is about an imag. glory, shame, and trials of everyday life. I highly recommend this engaging, artful book."

CHARLIE PEACOCK

(Record Producer, The Civil Wars, Holly Williams)

"*I have come that they may have life, and have it to the full.* This is Jesus's desire for each of us. Whether you are a creator, a parent, an activist, or you are harboring your own ambition for a fuller life, this book will help you discover God's calling for you to flourish."

RICH STEARNS

(President of World Vision US and author of
Unfinished and *The Hole in Our Gospel*)

"At its core *flourish* is a protest book against the million voices that tempt us to believe the work of our hearts and hands are of little consequence; a gentle call to listen instead to the still small voice that tells us to do, to make, to sing, to write, to be because we are and we matter."

JASON GRAY

(Recording Artist, Centricity Records)

"*flourish* is a book that calls out to the creative in each of us. Whether we craft with words, chords or a needle and thread, we can live a life of beauty and bring joy to those around us when we cultivate our gifts.

Staci challenged me to re-think how I see my own life of artistry, my passion for words and my desire to walk the path of beauty God has for me...she will do the same for you."

SUSANNA FOTH AUGHTMON,

(Author, *I Blame Eve*)

"Staci Frenes speaks the language of all of us who feel compelled to create, not only for others, but for the sake of our own heart-health. *flourish* is a poem of encouragement for reluctant creatives to dip deeply into the colors that define us and paint our souls onto the canvas for all to see."

TERRY ESAU

(Author, *Surprise Me*)

flourish

cultivate creativity
sow beauty
live in color

staci frenes

Printed in the United States of America
Library of Congress Cataloging-in-Publication Data

Frenes, Staci
Flourish — 1st edition
ISBN-13: 978-1502347039
ISBN-10: 1502347032

* Throughout this title there are underlined words which refer to
special links or comments noted within the rear NOTES section.

for dad

table of contents

Dear Reader,

I've been speaking at seminars, conferences and retreats about what it means to discover and live out our creative purpose, and as I've become familiar with what's most true and authentic to my life I've been inspired to write this book. It's filled with anecdotes and musings gleaned from my life as a songwriter, and also insight from friends, authors and thinkers I've been sparked by. All of it is filtered through the lens of my belief in a Master Creator, in whom all inspiration has its beginning and end.

To *flourish*, according to the dictionary, is "to grow and develop in a healthy vigorous way, especially as a result of a favorable environment." The insights and experiences I share in this book have helped me cultivate a life in which my gifts continue to find expression and grow, and I hope they'll do the same for you. You may find in these pages a starting point for your own creative journey, or encouragement for a long-forgotten one. It is my deepest desire that you'll be reminded that your life's work—whatever it is—matters. And that you'll discover the joy of sowing your *whole* self, with love, into the life God has given you and be amazed at the beauty that grows there.

As a songwriter, the most personal gift I can

share with you is the collection of songs I've written. You'll find stories about them and snippets of lyrics throughout the narrative. If you're reading this on an e-Reader there are links that will take you to the songs as you're reading. (Those links are also listed in the Notes section at the end of the book.) I hope you'll take full advantage of this feature and listen. I'd be over-the-moon happy to know you're enjoying my music while reading this!

At the end of each section I've posed some questions for you to reflect on, journal, discuss with friends, or — ideally — all of the above. Consider them my way of sitting down with you over coffee and talking about what you're reading. I want to know how some of these ideas and insights relate to your experience. Since I can't realistically meet ALL of you over coffee, feel free to email me with any thoughts you have about the book at staci@stacifrenes.com. I'd love to hear from you.

Thanks for reading,

staci frenes

throw yourself like seed

SEVERAL YEARS AGO ON A cold and rainy No-
vember afternoon my band and I were heading south
on Highway 5 into the heart of California's Central
Valley to do a concert in a small town several hours
from home. As usual, the four of us and all our musical gear were packed like sardines into our family's
'74 sky-blue VW "hippie bus" that leaked oil, had no
air-conditioning, no heat and no seat belts. But we'd
brought blankets to stay warm, and the CD player
was state-of-the-art, so we cruised along happily
enough, munching on junk food, laughing at each
others' dumb jokes and listening to music — *LOUD*.
Your basic Band Road Trip.

The concert venue was a church we'd never been
to which, as it turned out, was way off the beaten
path. The trip took longer than expected and we
were running late when we finally pulled up to the
building. Strangely, there were no other cars in the
lot. Usually there'd be at least a small team of folks
bustling around in preparation for a concert, so this
seemed odd, especially since we were getting close to
show time. We quickly unloaded our gear into the

auditorium and discovered the only ones there to greet us were the pastor of the church, his wife and their two young kids.

While we set up and sound checked with lightning-fast speed, I couldn't help feeling a sense of dread as I noticed no one else was arriving. The pastor kept throwing me apologetic looks, which didn't help my growing unease. The seven o'clock start time arrived and we agreed to wait a few minutes "to give people a chance to get here" (the pastor's slightly panic-laced suggestion), but as the clock crawled to seven-thirty the only bodies in that room were still just the four of them. They sat in the front row. The kids kicked their feet and punched each other out of boredom while the wife closely inspected a spot on the floor, never once making eye contact with me. My band paced around the back of the room restlessly, looking to me to make the call: *do we bail or go up there and play?* I wanted to click my heels three times and just disappear.

Finally, the pastor approached me, cleared his throat and said nervously, "I... uh ... thought we'd have a better turnout. You don't have to do this. You can just pack up and head home if you want." And in the beat of humiliating silence that followed, every ounce of me wanted to do just that. Clearly he—or someone—had monumentally dropped the ball on this event. And yet, some (crazy? determined?) part of me believed we'd come there to play music, so I smiled at the pastor, motioned to the guys and we went up and took our places on stage. We proceeded to do a full-blown concert with all the passion and energy we could muster. I think it surprised all of us that about halfway in we relaxed, made peace with the awkward situation and just had fun. When it was over we were rewarded with the sound of four sets of hands clapping and a long rainy drive home.

I can laugh about it now, but that night was rough. It played on my worst fears and seemed a fitting metaphor for the existential crisis I was fighting as that year came to a close. There was a nagging whispering in my ear I couldn't seem to silence that said *no one cares; your life's work doesn't matter.* As an independent singer/songwriter, I consider myself ridiculously blessed to be able to write, record and perform my own music for a living. And I'm grateful that most of the time there are more than four people who show up to my concerts. But like any job, there are aspects to what I do that wear me out and suck me dry, and after a long discouraging winter I found myself in a season where the rewards seemed too few and far between for the amount of energy I put in. In essence, I felt like I was singing to an empty room.

Soon after that night, I bought a book of poetry as I was looking for solace from my depression. (Some see a therapist, some take vacations; I take the cheaper route and turn to poetry.) I was trying to get ramped up, psyched up and geared up for a new year of work and life, and the transition wasn't going well. I felt fragmented and severely lacking in motivation. Like anyone, I desperately wanted to know that my life's work mattered to the universe and to the people in my world; that I was more than a speck of dust floating through the atmosphere. I wanted to leave a trace—some kind of imprint that was uniquely my own. But that December I felt like a fading vapor trail across the sky. Insignificant. Forgettable.

One poem in particular from that little book grabbed my heart in the first line: *Shake off this sadness and recover your spirit.* I needed to do that, badly, but didn't know how. The poem suggested *turn to the work,* over and over. Which didn't make sense at first. After all, wasn't it my work that was draining, exhausting and discouraging me? I read it again, and wondered if what the poet called "work" wasn't actually the mundane, clock-punching, or even money-making aspects of it, but rather the things I give my *full self* to—the people and projects I invest in wholly—heart, personality, beliefs, and talents.

When I thought back over my discouraging year, I realized I'd lost sight of that particular perspective on my work, and seemed instead to be looking for a pat on the back and a paycheck. I was counting and measuring what was coming in, rather than pouring out what I'd been given. How many people were showing up to concerts? How many CDs had I sold?

How many gigs did I have on my calendar? How many Facebook likes, Twitter followers? It was unraveling me from the inside and I wanted to *recover my spirit* like the poem promised. I wanted to find my joy and sense of purpose again. To know my worth apart from the value others placed on it.

Maybe that's why I decided to stay and do a concert for that embarrassed pastor and his family that night. Maybe I saw clearly—in that split second moment of decision, anyway—that doing what I'm designed and called to do wasn't about how many people were in the room to witness or appreciate it. Nor was it about whether my expectations were met or my agenda accomplished. Up on that stage playing music I discovered it *was* possible to experience the joy inherent in giving myself fully to the opportunities God placed in my path, no matter how big or small. I actually *could* feel pleasure in creating something beautiful and sharing it, without caring what I got in return.

I believe the tears, sweat and blood I've poured into my work over the years have been giving life to something bigger than me, more important than my happiness on a given day. And my hope is that it continues to encourage, comfort, and inspire someone else. I won't ever fully comprehend the scope or impact of my life's work, but I can recognize that it has worth and that it is a work *only* I can do, with my unique set of relationships, opportunities and talents.

In that recognition comes the strength to gather myself, shake off my sadness and recover my spirit. Just like the poem says.

Throw Yourself Like Seed

Shake off this sadness, and recover your spirit.
Sluggish you will never see the wheel of fate
That brushes your heel as it turns going by,
The man who wants to live is the man
in whom life is abundant.
Now you are only giving food to that final pain
Which is slowly winding you in the nets of death,
But to live is to work, and the only thing which lasts
Is the work; start then, turn to the work.
Throw yourself like seed as you walk,
and into your own field,
Don't turn your face for that would be to turn it to death,
And do not let the past weigh down your motion.
Leave what's alive in the furrow, what's dead in yourself,
For life does not move in the same
way as a group of clouds;
From your work you will be able one
day to gather yourself.

~ Miguel De Unamuno ~

creative identity:
gather your seeds

nana and me

… all men and women are entrusted with the
task of crafting their own life …
to make of it a work of art, a masterpiece.
– Pope John Paul II, Letter to Artists

SATURDAYS WERE ALWAYS THE BUSIEST in my Nana's little dress shop. Pin cushion on her wrist, one or two pins in her mouth at the ready, tape measure around her neck, she was either chalking a hem, attaching a row of ruffles to a neckline or pressing wrinkles out of something stretched across the ironing board. Against one wall stood a clothing rack with six or seven plastic-encased articles ready for pick up, and draped over a chair next to Nana's white Singer lay a pile of the day's work yet to be done: blouses, pants, dresses, skirts, blazers all loosely pinned or otherwise marked in some code only she understood.

Nana, Viola Matilda Anderson, my grandmother on my mother's side, was a professional seamstress in my hometown of Grand Forks, North Dakota. Her shop, a renovated room in my grandparents' little house, was a perpetual flurry of spinning spools of multi-colored thread and the familiar whir and hum of her trusty sewing machine. It was my favorite Saturday morning hangout. I loved being right in the middle of the sounds, the smells, and all there was to see in that little dress shop because it was all Nana— her work, her world, her laughter and her energy. She was the most creative, passionate, immensely talented person I'd ever been around.

Everyone for miles around knew Nana was the best in town. People—mostly women in those days— came to her at all hours of the day and from all walks of life. She tailored their pantsuits, hemmed their skirts, designed and sewed their prom dresses, Easter outfits, and even their wedding gowns. My mom tells stories of coming home from class with ideas in her head for a dress to wear to the upcoming school dance. Mom would describe how the neckline should scoop this way, the bodice hug here, how far out the skirt should flounce when she twirled…and that's all Nana needed. She'd plant herself at the sewing machine and stay there until the dress blossomed beneath her expert hands—just as my mom had pictured it.

Mom wasn't the only beneficiary of Nana's talent. I remember her making lots of outfits for me as a kid. I'd get ideas for outfits watching my favorite show, *The Brady Bunch*—worn by the goddess of all cool TV chicks in the 70's, Marcia Brady. Or, I'd see a picture of something cute in *Teen Beat* magazine and beg Nana to make it for me. And she would. It's a testament to her skill that I wore those outfits well into my junior high years with none of the usual reluctance associated with wearing something "homemade from a relative." (Hello, holiday sweaters?) Her clothes had bona fide department store legitimacy, and I felt special and stylish wearing them.

Unexpectedly, when I was 11 years old my parents packed up the house and we moved from Grand Forks, North Dakota clear across the country to Alameda, California. Think Beverly Hillbillies but in a wood-paneled station wagon. They wanted a new start, a clean break from their Midwestern roots. Me? Not so much. I missed my friends horribly and hated my parents for moving so far away from all that was dear and familiar. The only bright spots those first few months were the care packages from Nana. She must've known how lonely I was because she often sent me a special outfit or skirt, hand-sewn, of course, with love. One in particular I wore for my sixth grade school picture consisted of a polyester tunic and matching bell-bottomed pants in a pink paisley print. (Don't judge, I was a child of the 70's.) It suited me perfectly. Wearing that outfit felt like a warm hug from Nana.

Looking back, I wore that outfit and so many others she created for me with the secretly proud and delightful sense that they were one-of-a-kind, made just for me. If she had sewn tags into the outfits they would have read something like *I made this for you, because I love you!* That's how personal her clothes felt. It's as though she gave her very self to me — to all of us who wore her clothes — in the pieces she created. I felt richer in love for being able to experience her spirit in this tangible way.

I like to think Nana was the first example I saw of a "working artist." She wouldn't have used that term — she probably would have laughed at such a fancy title. But she had the precision, professionalism and panache of an artist, stamping every item of clothing that left her little shop with her personal imprint of excellence. She had a certain way of cocking her head sideways as she looked at a dress or pair of pants she'd worked on: it was as though she didn't want one single detail to escape her so she'd peer at it askance, daring even one tiny flaw to bring itself to her eagle-eye attention. Rarely did she find one; she was that skilled at her craft.

Nana worked at what she loved, creating and sewing clothes almost every day of her life, and it was her immense talent and professionalism that allowed her to make a living at it. Sewing for people fueled her emotional tank, it kept her up at all hours, it made her a little loony during busy seasons, but I know now it infused her life with a sense of purpose and deep fulfillment. Nana was never happier and more focused than when she was sitting at her sewing machine, knee-deep in fabric, thread and deadlines.

I sometimes think about how many of the clothes Nana made outlived her. They were worn and re-worn, passed down to daughters, nieces, grandkids, neighbors, and maybe even a few Goodwill racks where they were bought by housewives on a budget or college students hunting down vintage treasures. I imagine brides who nervously walked down church aisles in Nana's dresses, babies who squirmed in her christening gowns, and my mom as a teen in one of her dreamt-up, specially made party dresses, dancing with the handsome shy boy who later became her husband, and my dad. Each person lived a different life, experiencing the full gamut of human emotions wearing a garment that was cut, stitched and pressed by Nana's own hands. Her works of art stretched beyond the limits of her 88 years.

When she died, we discovered Nana had written detailed instructions about her funeral service on the inside of her Bible. I was to sing her two favorite hymns: "At the Cross" and "In the Garden." I'd sung for Nana a million times over the years, but as I sat down at the piano that afternoon I wondered how I'd make it through these songs I'd been hearing *her* humming at the sewing machine as far back as I could remember. My voice cracked and I had to choke down a sob in a couple of places, but I sang from my heart with all the love I had for my joyful spirited Nana. It was the best gift I had to offer her.

Two generations later, I, too, find myself a working artist, creating for a living. My tools are much different than Nana's; truthfully, I'm completely useless with a sewing machine or even a needle and thread. I'm most comfortable with my guitar and the melodies and words that I shape into songs. Fast, upbeat joyous ones and mournful, contemplative moody ones — I feel them well up inside of me, needing to be birthed. Songs are the language I speak, the thoughts I think, they are the way I receive and give back to the world around me. When I write and sing my songs, I'm more grounded and content than when I'm doing any other thing. I feel a kind of transcendent timeless connection to something bigger than me; as though what I am doing matters in a way I can't quantify or explain.

I've recorded and released several CDs and performed in concert halls, coffeehouses, stadiums, churches, amusement parks, television studios, radio stations, community centers and anywhere else I've been invited. I've written songs for other artists who have recorded and found their way onto countless stages and radio airwaves; I've licensed songs to hundreds of photographers and videographers which have been featured in videos and websites all over the country; I've had songs playing on airlines and major television shows and films. I've written songs for non-profit organizations, hospitals and TV commercials, for too many weddings, funerals, church worship services to count, anniversaries and birthdays. You name it. I've written a song or two about it.

It's daunting, and humbling to think about how the songs I've written have left my hands and traveled to places I will never see or know, to live a life of their own with meanings as different as each listener who hears them. I sometimes think of them like the clothes Nana made for so many people throughout the years of her life. She offered them the best gift she had—the work of her hands, which they wore and made their own. I hope that others can hear something of their own story in some of my songs and feel understood; or hear comfort and hope in the words I write and feel less alone.

This kindred creative spirit I share with my nana has little to do with the kind of art we each make, and one isn't more or less important or worthy. It has to do with the love we share of expressing something new—shaping it, tweaking it, playing with it until it starts to please us, starts to feel like an authentic and unique creation, unlike anything else we've seen or heard. We enjoy working at our creativity, because it's something only we can do, and in the stretching, cutting and pinching of the materials under our hands we begin to feel our art do its work on us, too.

We find out who we are and what we love.

calling it good

If you want to know what you are here to do, look around
you, at the life you already have …
the work that is truly yours
is the life that is truly yours.
– Roger Housden (poet)

AS TALENTED AS MY NANA was, I know that my
desire to create goes back much farther than just two
generations. Since I've been able to form words and
hear melodies, I've wanted to give them shapes and
rhythms and make them into songs. I've never understood where it came from, exactly. Neither of my
parents is particularly musical, and although my
mom took piano lessons as a kid, she'll be the first to
tell you she can't carry a tune to save her life. But I
could — and from the time I could make noise, I wanted to sing and make up my own songs. I don't ever
remember consciously *choosing* whether or not to
give expression to the words and melodies that began to form inside of me, welling up to the point of
almost spilling over; I just knew they needed releas-

ing.

There's no taking credit for the origins of my own creativity. I believe the desire and the ability to make music were etched into my DNA by God's own hand long before I recognized it or called it *songwriting*. Think about the countless other forms of creative expression we first discover in ourselves. From an early age we desire to build, explore, draw, dance, make up stories and shape materials using our imaginations and whatever we've got on hand—without any coaching or prompting from grownups. As we grow and begin to experience the full range of what it is to be human, our longing to find an expression for that experience deepens and continues to search for creative outlets. We are created to create. One of my favorite writers on this subject, Madeline L'Engle, in her book *Walking on Water*, says, "*God is constantly creating in us, through us and with us.*"

God *is* the original Artist and Creator. Look around. We're surrounded by natural beauty that defies capturing with words: majestic landscapes, vast blue oceans and every kind and color of living thing our wildest dreams can conjure. The One responsible has been painting a different sunset every night since time began. He scatters billions of stars like glitter across the black firmament. Galaxies of light and mass pulse and spin in the night sky. The Master of epic-scale creation, yet exquisite in every infinitesimal detail—even the unfolding petals of a fragrant rose bear His imprint. Unparalleled, extravagant beauty fills our senses from any angle and every viewpoint of this untamed and mysterious universe we call home. It's His handiwork, His show.

No wonder poet Annie Dillard writes, "*Creation need not play to an empty house.*" God's brilliant artwork is always on display and free to anyone who wants to see it. The least we can do is pay attention once in a while and allow it to take our breath away.

The curtain rises
The show begins
A field of wildflowers dances in the wind
Majestic thunder
Clouds roll by
Lightning cuts a path across an indigo sky
Ooh, ah
You take my breath away
Ooh, ah
The beauty you create
Is matchless, magnificent
Your artistry
Always leaves me
Breathless

("Breathless" by Staci Frenes
© 2012 Stone's Throw Music/ASCAP)

Genesis tells us that for six days God performed the miracle play of *Creation* in the theater of the cosmos, and near the end of the unfolding drama, like a consummate showman, He saved his best for last. His most complex, multi-dimensioned creation: a human being. He drew the blueprint for the intricacies of a heart that beats blood and oxygen through the veins of even the tiniest newborn baby. Intelligent design, indeed. Thumbprints and snowflakes only tell half the story of how *fearfully and wonderfully* we are made. Elegant and fragile, beautiful and complex, we bear a distinct honor among all other created beings in that we are made in His image.

God said, 'Let us make mankind in our image, after our likeness' ... And God saw everything that He had made, and behold it was very good. (Genesis 1:26, 31)

Creating is the first thing we see God doing in scripture. I imagine Him rolling up His sleeves, shaping the misty black chaos into day and night, land and sky, and setting the sun and moon in place. From time to time during this art fest He steps back, squints His eye, cocks His head and says *it is good.* He sees worth, beauty, *goodness* in the work of His hands. I can almost picture Nana sitting back from her sewing machine, holding a dress she's finished up to the light, turning it around a few times in her hands and declaring in her Scandinavian accent, "Yah, it's good!" I don't think of any of my songs as technically perfect, but there's something undoubtedly good about a song that manages to come out the way I hear it in my imagination.

It makes sense that because we are made in God's own likeness — with minds and hearts to imagine and dream — we share the desire to create something of our own. Each of us is a kind of working artist in our own fashion. With a unique set of talents and tools, we create in a variety of ways: compose music, design web sites, write stories, choreograph dances, and photograph people and places. Drawn to mediums as diverse as our personalities, backgrounds and environments; we work with clay, with numbers or HTML code, with images, sounds and words in a way that reflects our interests and talents. Some of us do this creative work for a living, but for most of us our creativity exists in a different economy altogether — one in which there are returns richer and deeper than paychecks and status. Creativity awakens in us that innate and deep-seated desire to make something and call it good.

I've heard people refer to their area of creativity as a hobby, as though it exists only in small, compartmentalized pockets and gets let out at a scrapbooking or dance class. I beg to differ. Or at least to suggest that there's a difference between the once-in-a-while-activity you do that feels more "artsy" than your real job, and what, in fact, is your unique set of talents, skills, and personality seeking creative expression. While it may not be your *career* path, creativity is a *soul* path that nourishes and massages the stiff, worn out muscles of clock-punching mundane industry work. In our creative endeavors we are re-freshed; we use a different part of our brain; we manage to find ways to express what in our normal workday world feels inexpressible.

I took an art history class in college and learned about the great painter, Pablo Picasso, and his fa-mous Blue Period. Between 1901 and 1904, following the suicide of a dear friend, Picasso painted only in blue and blue-green tones to reflect his grief; most of the subject matter somber and gloomy. The public rejected many of the paintings at the time — people thought the work was too depressing. By 1905 he'd moved on to his Rose Period, creating paintings which were immediately popular; but some of the Blue Period pieces would later become his most sought after and valuable work. As a college student sitting in that dark auditorium seeing some of these Blue Period paintings and trying to understand the complex heart of this great artist, I was grateful that from such a painful season of life Picasso left this hauntingly beautiful body of work for the rest of us.

When we're feeling something deeply — grief or joy; love or despair — we want to find a way to ex-press it in order to share the depth of that emotion or experience with someone else. The search for our own authentic form of expression in any given mo-ment is also the search for who we are in that moment, and what we want to share of ourselves with the world. Picasso's paintings during that season of his life emerged in blues and greens, mirroring the despair he felt at the loss of his friend. As an experienced and gifted artist he was able to shape the chaos of his own pain into beauty; painting his grief onto the canvas.

The first-century Saint Irenaeus said, "The glory of God is man fully alive." Maybe being *fully alive* to ourselves, to God, and to those around us involves doing what is uniquely ours to do. It means painting in greens, singing the blues or fashioning our thoughts and moods into the various colors, shapes and forms that emerge from our creativity. It means finding expression for the ideas that well up inside us, and then living them out loud in creative ways that bring us joy, give us purpose, and bring beauty into the world. Doing work that we can call 'good'. It means feeling what God must have felt when he was flinging stars from his fingertips or breathing life into Adam. Fully alive, we reflect the artistry of the One who created us.

Fully alive and breathing
The greatest work of art is all humanity
Each of us on this moving canvas
Reflects a different stroke of the Artist's brush

("Picasso's Blues" by Staci Frenes © 2004 Staci Frenes Stone's Throw Music/ASCAP)

talents

Open up your hands
Take what the giver has for you
To harvest and to plant
Faithful in the work he's called you to
– from "<u>Only Love Lives On</u>"
by Staci Frenes, Nate Sabin

LAST SUMMER I DECIDED TO get my exercise groove on every morning before it got too hot. Nothing too crazy—I power walked, or at least, that's what I called it to make it sound official—and from the walking path I could see the backyards of several houses that backed up to it. I saw one man in particular about the same time every day. He was cultivating a small vegetable garden in a corner of his lot. The area had to be cleared, tilled, and the soil treated before he seeded the neat rows he had dug. He was a skilled gardener; he knew where to plant which seeds where so they'd have room to spread out and get sunlight as they grew. He shored up the plants that started to droop, kept the weeds out, and watered everything regularly throughout the hot summer. I watched these tiny green shoots grow into a healthy, abundant garden.

He had four children out there "helping" him many days—none of them looked over five years old!—digging, planting and watering, but mostly running around and playing on the swings he'd hung from tree branches nearby. And while I'm sure his kids learned a few tips about gardening, it was obvious they just loved being outside with their daddy, and he seemed delighted having them near while he worked. By the end of the season, this little garden yielded an impressive crop: tomatoes, zucchini, cucumbers, corn, yellow squash, and more. There was enough fruit from his labor for his family, friends and probably several neighbors to enjoy.

There were aspects to how this father went about tending his garden that resonated deeply with me about the way we're to approach our own lives—particularly with regard to the use of our gifts and talents. His diligence and attentiveness were admirable, and so was his ability to work the difficult soil of this region and get such good results. The seeds he planted were well-chosen for our climate, and he didn't use a lot of expensive, fancy tools for the job. He made it all look so simple and really, it wasn't a huge spectacle of a garden. I'm sure many walkers and bikers along that path passed by it without a glance. But I saw his handiwork, and it was both beautiful and functional.

I think of that father as each one of us, responsible for tending the garden of our own life — the friends, family, career and community where we live. The size and span of our gardens may differ, but using the tools best suited for our work, we each to some degree invest the seeds of our time and our unique talents, sowing them into the people and projects we care about. When we do so diligently and wisely, what grows are relationships, opportunities, and rewards that fulfill and enrich everyone involved. That little garden seemed to illustrate for me a life richly invested with love for people and for one's life work; a life abundant in fruit and in joy.

If we want to cultivate a rich creative life, maybe we should start with the simple question: what are the seeds I have in my hands to plant? What are the distinct talents or skills with which I invest in my own life? Some of us are looking at the wildly overgrown plot of land that's to become our garden, and we've never really assessed what our creative skills or talents are, much less how to use them. In fact, we've wondered many times whether we've been short-changed in the talent department — especially if we don't see ourselves as particularly "gifted" or "creative" in some of the more obvious ways.

In the Parable of the Talents, like any good story, we find insight about the choices we make — specifically, as they relate to the gifts we're given and

what we do with them. In the version of the story
found in Matthew 25 three servants are given a different number of talents by their king while he's
away. The two servants given the most talents invest
them well and double the amounts by the time the
king returns, for which he praises and rewards them.
The servant given the least amount buries his talent
for safekeeping while the king is away, for which he
is harshly chastised and banished when the king returns. His one talent is then given to the servant with
the most—making the point that those who are responsible with much will be given more, while those
who don't use what they're given will lose it.

A couple of core truths in this story strike me
right away. One is that all three servants are given
something with which to work—to invest and do
business in the king's absence. The obvious point is
that we're all entrusted with some measure of God's
resources, tangible and intangible, including particular gifts and talents that are suited to our personalities and strengths. Scripture tells us *every good and
perfect gift* comes from God (James 1:17) and that the
gifts of God *can never be withdrawn* (Romans 11:29).
Yours and mine are no exception. Whether or not
we're using them, or even fully recognize them, we
have been given gifts by God that are good; perfect,
even, and non-refundable. It's this bedrock premise
on which this story relies, and on which our discus-
sion of cultivating a creative life rests as well: we all

have something of value to work with.

Something else fairly obvious in this story seems, on the surface, unfair. The three servants are each given a different number of talents. A talent in those days represented a significant amount of money, perhaps as much as several years' wages. One servant is given ten talents, another five and the third servant given just one. I can't help but wonder why is one given more? Some justification seems to be in order, to my way of thinking. Yet the only explanation given is the small phrase, *each* (was given an amount) *according to his ability*. Whatever the reason, and however arbitrary and random it may seem to us, the parable suggests that there are some that have more to start out with.

Some of us get stuck at this point in our own stories and never move beyond it. We struggle in a perpetual state of comparison with others. If we spend any time at all on social media sites (Facebook, Twitter, Instagram) it's easy to find plenty of people who have more stuff, more talent, more opportunities than we do. If we're honest about how many times we've compared ourselves and come away feeling less-than or short-changed we may be surprised at the discontentment bubbling beneath our surface. We stack ourselves up against each other in every category from looks and possessions to spiritual maturity and careers. And when we come up lacking, it just doesn't seem fair.

Fair is a concept we seem to learn early on, isn't it? My son, Zach, and my daughter, Abby, were born on the same day — August 31st, three years apart. (I know, right? What are the chances?) When they were toddlers we'd have one big party to celebrate both of their birthdays, but as they got older they wanted to have their own parties with their own friends and their own cakes. So, we started having two parties, sometimes on the same day, (which was as insane as you might imagine) and sometimes a day or week apart. There were years when one of them wanted a big party with lots of friends, and another wanted just a family dinner with their favorite meal. We'd do whatever the birthday boy and girl wanted, but always tried to be as fair as possible, spending close to the same amount of money on their gifts and parties so neither would feel slighted. Trust me, *they paid attention* and held us to it.

When Zach graduated from high school, his birthday gift from us that summer was a MacBook computer. It was one of the only times we spent a lot more money on him than we did on Abby. We expected fierce repercussions from her, so we had a little preemptive talk, explaining that her brother was older, had accomplished something important and would need a computer for college classes he was taking in the fall. He was at a different stage in his life, we explained, and the laptop was an appropriate reward as well as tool for him. She got it, and we breathed a sigh of relief, glad not to have a full-scale revolt on our hands.

You and I have been given good gifts perfectly suited to our abilities and personalities. Along with those come opportunities unique to our circumstances. Consider every door that's been opened to you because of your talents: a job offer, a spot on the team, a book deal, a treasured relationship, or a position of leadership. If we measure our own value based on what others have, we cripple not only our creativity but also our core sense of self-worth. While we *look on the outward appearance* (1 Samuel 16:7), God searches our hearts and sees our willingness to serve, love, risk and invest the gifts we're given.

Shaking our fist in the air yelling, "It's not fair!" doesn't change the fact that what we've been given may not be equal to what others have been given. It does, however, take our eyes off the far more important matter of what resources, talents, and opportunities God *has* given us, and what we're doing with those things. Before we can move ahead in our own creative life, we need to first come to peace with the seeming inequity, (but reality nonetheless) that some may have more; ultimately trusting that God knows exactly who we are and what we need to live fulfilled, abundant lives.

children at play

Adults follow paths. Children explore.
– Neil Gaiman (novelist)

AT THE BEACH A WHILE back, I watched a group of little kids make a sand castle while their mom, reading a short distance away, kept an eye on them. They worked non-stop for at least two hours, dumping wet sand from a bucket, shaping it with shovels and hand pats, and making regular trips to the water to fill the moat they'd dug around the castle. The whole operation was conducted with squeals and giggles and the occasional shriek when a wave snuck up too close to the walls. As the sun started to set and Mama called them to come and gather their things, they groaned in protest, yelling back, "Can we *please* stay and finish our work?" I had to smile at the word "work" and wondered when was the last time I had so much fun making something that I completely lost track of time? When was the last time I used my gifts the way I did when I was a kid—just for the joy of it?

A big part of cultivating creativity is playing again the way we did when we were kids. If I want to remember what playing feels like, I hang out with kids for a while and it starts coming back to me: how the point is to have fun, not to compete with others; how it's okay to make up the games, and therefore the rules, as I go; how there's no such thing as making mistakes; how everything else gets tuned out while I focus on the moment. Most of all, how it's impossible to be self-conscious and have fun at the same time. Children have an innocent, vulnerable way of forgetting about themselves when they're engrossed in making up a game or role-playing or any kind of art making. There's no shrinking back or comparing of skills, they're too busy diving in headlong, because what matters is not that they've got sand on their faces, or that they're following the right blueprint for the castle, but that they're having fun making it.

My earliest memories of singing were during car trips in the back seat of my parents' lime green AMC Gremlin. My poor dad was color blind, and family legend has it that somehow he thought the car was a shade of beige—at least that's the story he told my mom in an attempt to talk her down when she saw him drive home from the car dealership. My 70's post-hippie folks blasted 8-tracks of artists like John Denver, Simon and Garfunkel, Elton John, and The Carpenters in that Gremlin. I sang along in the

backseat at the top of my lungs like nobody's business. Nothing made me happier than a long drive
and lots of 8-tracks of the soft-rock variety. (Yes,
those are my musical roots you're seeing, friends.)

I learned to experiment with my voice and
taught myself to sing harmonies during those drives.
It was like a game. I'd listen to the lead singers and
try to imitate them until we fused perfectly into a
single-sounding voice. I'd copy the airy, breathy way
they sang the soft parts and the throaty growls of the
sexy or rockin' parts. Once I got bored with that I'd
search above or below the melody to find a note that
sounded like it blended nicely and didn't clash. It
took me lots of tries and wrong notes but I got pretty
good at singing harmony. My sister and brother and
I would sit squashed together, cruisin' in the backseat of that green Gremlin, and while they moaned
and asked if we were there yet, I became what I
thought was a pretty fantastic singer. Nobody taught
me the rules of how to sing a third above or below
the note, or open my diaphragm for longer notes … I
just figured it out having fun with it.

My love of all things music was closely matched
by my passion for words. I wrote poems and stories
and diary entries as soon as I learned how to form
sentences. My Nana had a Wall of Fame leading
down the stairs to her shop full of drawings and poems of her nine grandchildren. It was my life's weekly goal to see one of my poems up on Nana's wall.

One in particular I still remember writing, then re-copying in dark ink and my fanciest third grade cursive writing, began with this stunning couplet (dedicated to Nana, of course):

> *you're awfully sweet*
> *you smell like meat*

I know. You're wondering how I followed that amazing opener. Suffice it to say, I dazzled my way onto that Wall of Fame week after week with beauties like those. I liked playing with words the way some kids play with building blocks or clay: rhyming, shaping, and arranging them on a page in ways I thought enhanced their meaning and made them seem poetic. Nana gushed over them, but so did others—clients, friends, even my cousins (the competition!) admitted I had a knack for words.

I was about 12 years old when my two chief loves—words and music—collided in the form of songwriting. After a few piano and guitar lessons I started cranking out songs left and right. They came spontaneously, bubbling up when I sat down at the piano, or with a guitar. The delight I felt at crafting words and phrases into melodies with chord patterns was a world of wonder to me. I wrote songs every waking moment. I sang in talent shows and entered poetry contests in junior high. All through high school I sang and wrote songs with my friend Jill in our self-named duo, *Stained Glass.* We played guitars, wore matching plaid vest-and-skirt outfits and rocked big 80's perms like they were going out of style. (Which, thankfully, they did.) We hopped on cable cars and Muni buses and sang our hearts out around the city of San Francisco. We had a blast.

Psychologists tell us there are stages of self-awareness we pass through on the way to adulthood. The younger we are, the less conscious we are of what everyone else thinks of us. As toddlers we pretty much march to our own drumbeat, but by the time we're rounding six or seven we're starting to catch on to social cues about what's acceptable behavior. From then on, those cues become more sophisticated, and we find ourselves for the most part, acting accordingly. Playing, which comes naturally when we've no idea if we look or sound silly, often gets lost in the process. So much of what fueled my early musical confidence had nothing to do with what "the professionals" thought (that would come later); it had everything to do with the joy I felt while doing it.

I love playful people; probably because they help me not be so serious—which I confess I'm sometimes accused of. Playful people don't take themselves too seriously, which is the *point* of playing, right? To have fun. To laugh. To keep things light. If we can create some time to "play" at our work like those kids I saw with their sand castle, we might be surprised by not only the delight we discover in it but also the productivity. It's the kind of productivity that happens when we explore, risk, or try new things that lead to discoveries: find new directions to follow and the wealth of ideas we find along those unexpected tangents. We don't get to those tangential discoveries without the exploration, and exploration means getting off of our beaten paths.

My friend, Faith, is a graphic artist whose list of clients includes big corporations like Target and Home Depot, as well as independent musicians like me. She's designed the artwork for several of my CDs, and one I'm especially crazy about is the _Wise Men and Angels_ Christmas album design. Two of the main images Faith used were paper figures made from Christmas carol sheet music steeped in tea overnight to give it a vintage look, then folded into the shapes of an angel and a star. I remember her describing the process as kind of a hit-and-miss operation, with a few of the sheets not quite turning out right, but as she kept playing with the figures and the coloring of the tea eventually she got the look she wanted. In almost every project she's designed for me, the process seems to involve experimenting with her hands elbow-deep in paint, flour paste or some other goop, which, to me, sounds like play. I love that about Faith's work.

While she admits she doesn't get to play nearly as much as she'd like at her "day job," certain projects Faith does for her own enjoyment rather than a client's approval are important in helping her "keep a pocket of self-expression sacred," she says. She calls it art camp: doodling on napkins, painting late at night in her basement. For her it's therapy … those times when she allows herself to let go and create from her heart. It shows in her finished products — the design work she's done for me is fresh, often whimsical and unexpected. It doesn't look like anyone else's work.

I heard someone say that art begins as play. I'd add dreaming, imagining, exploring — all the things children seem to do without nudging from us grown-ups. Recover your creative joy by remembering what you loved to do as a child, and do more of it.

remembering what we forgot

Every child is an artist. The problem is how to remain an artist once he grows up.
– Pablo Picasso (painter)

SOMEWHERE IN MY EARLY JUNIOR high years I had a short but defining conversation I'll never forget. At the time, I was babysitting for a family with two adorable little boys whose parents had an air of worldly sophistication bordering on movie-star status. My sister and I both had a crush on the whole family. I felt shy and tongue-tied around them, especially the father. Something about Mr. Soltana made me feel naïve and invisible. Late night car rides when he took me home after babysitting — just the two of us — were excruciatingly awkward. Ten minutes felt like an hour.

One night during one of those drives, Mr. Soltana, who'd recently heard me sing at an event, turned his megawatt attention on me and asked suddenly, "So … this singing thing. What are you going to do with it?"

I had no clue how to answer that question; especially not there, in front of him. I probably cleared my throat a few times to buy some time, then I mumbled something like, "Um … I'm not sure yet?"

Mr. Soltana kept going. "Because you're good, you know that? Real good. You could probably go anywhere, do anything with that talent. And no offense—singing Christian music is fine—but you could do a lot better than that. Go to Hollywood or LA or someplace. Get discovered. Go big time."

I think by then I'd turned into a sweaty red beet. Some part of me knew he was paying me a compliment, but another part of me, for reasons I couldn't really articulate, felt massively confused. Was he implying that *real* talent belonged in the *real* world of professional entertainment? That the only way to validate my musical gift was to "go big time" with it? And what did going "big time" even mean? My teenaged self had no idea. I thought I was just supposed to have fun with this whole singing thing.

For years I replayed that conversation in my head. It seemed to represent an ongoing internal struggle I had going into my adult years. It's one I think many of us have when we reach a pivotal age where we think we need to *get serious* about our talent. We ask ourselves: What exactly am I supposed to *do* with this gift? What are the proper steps I should be taking to make it legitimate—something that people like Mr. Soltana would respect and approve of? Am I supposed to make money with it? Do I get an education for it? Must I achieve some level of status or fame with it? In the early years of discovering my voice and my songwriting I had no idea about any of that.

In their book, *Art & Fear*, David Bayles and Ted Orland tell a story of painter and art instructor, Howard Ikemoto, whose seven-year-old daughter asked him one day what he did at work. He told her he worked at the college and that his job was to teach people how to draw. She stared back at him, incredulous, and said, "You mean they forgot?" Many of us do "forget" what we knew as children. We unlearn some of that natural follow-your-gut spontaneity and raw emotion, and instead stay inside the lines of rules and constraints we think characterize a more serious approach to our craft. We check ourselves against societal or self-imposed standards. We tone down and tame the wildness of our instincts. We gradually move from art as play to playing it safe.

If we can dig back into our most pleasurable memories of the things we loved doing before anyone labeled our "gift" or "talent" as such, before anyone told us there were rules to it; before we discovered there were others who do it differently, or better, or make more money at it; before we learned that not everyone would like what we do. If we can remember back before all of that, to when it came as naturally to us as breathing, we might have the kind of courage Hemingway talks about when he says we should *...acquire the courage to do what children did when they knew nothing.*

I remember watching my kids play one morning in a park when they were just toddlers. I was sitting on a bench nearby, close enough to see them but far enough to give them space to run around and do their thing without me shadowing every move. They lost sight of me once in a while, I'm sure, going in and out of the play structure, swooshing down the slide, hanging from the monkey bars. I was ready to pounce if it looked like they might fall or get pushed around, but they played on fearlessly without a care in the world.

Sitting there watching them I thought about my life, and my career, especially. I felt ancient, weighed down with so much worry and anxiety about the future. Worried about whether things were going as well as they ought to be, given how old I was. Wondering if I was doing everything right, and being as productive and smart as I should be with the opportunities I had. Despairing that I had no way of knowing what tomorrow would hold and wanting so desperately to have some kind of control over that. But I couldn't, any more than my kids could know what the next moment held on that playground.

The difference was they weren't worried about it. They were running around, screaming and laughing up a storm. I wondered when it was I'd forgotten how to have fun in my creative life. It seemed like what I once loved so much about making music was overshadowed now by expectations and anxiety. I wasn't letting myself just play anymore. Ultimately, I didn't trust things would fall into place unless I was worrying and stressing about them 24/7. I needed to let go of all that worry if I was ever going to recover my childlike ability to play at my work.

I wrote this song, "I Suppose", about that day in the park. It's an ongoing reminder to me to let go of what I can't control about my life, my career, and my kids.

I Suppose

My children play in a world of danger
And never worry about a thing
Not tryin' to peek around every corner
Perfectly fearless and naive
As only carefree hearts can be
I suppose it only goes to show
We're maybe not supposed to know
How life unfolds
Try to just be brave and turn the page
Baby everything will be okay
Trust and just let go
I suppose

("I Suppose" by Staci Frenes, Nate Sabin © 2008 Stone's Throw Music/ASCAP Lorilu Music/ASCAP)

Hemingway's right: approaching our talents with the open-hearted simplicity of a child again does take courage. It means trying new things at the risk of failing and looking unprofessional or paddling against the current of popular opinion or industry trends. It means allowing ourselves to hope like a child again—even when our past disappointments tell us it's foolish to do so. It takes a conscious choice to open ourselves up to new possibilities in our creativity—possibilities we gave up on or dismissed as impossible or silly or a waste of time as we gradually "grew up" and steeled our hearts against such frivolous dreams.

Hope is easy to forget. It's sort of the banana peel of emotions; once you put all your weight on it you risk falling and getting hurt. Yet hope and imagination are pillars of childlike creativity. I heard a pastor and speaker, Al Andrews, once say that hope has two unpleasant companions—wait and ache—and as the crescendo of hope grows and is not realized, pain also grows. So we either ignore hope, denying its existence, or we keep moving because if we stop it hurts, and the fragile hope we've taken such great care to keep tender crystallizes into cynicism. We become bitter, hard. I know what this feels like; I've been disappointed too many times to count in the course of my independent music career. Albums I thought would sell well didn't. Songs I thought would go more places, touch more people, slipped into obscurity. Dreams for a national tour with other artists I'd admired and worked with never materialized.

So if hope exists to set us up for either bitterness or disappointment, why hope? Al Andrews believes — and so do I — we hope because we're designed to yearn and long for a reunion with God and all that He is that we are not yet: perfect love, holiness, unspoiled beauty. We hope for many of the same reasons we create: it gives us glimpses into what could be. Art deepens that yearning and paints pictures of what we cannot yet fully see, like children building the sand castle they see in their imaginations.

Reconnect with that part of yourself that first fell in love with the joy of "making stuff" before you learned the rules and expectations and roadblocks that so often discourage and stifle our creative impulses. Abandon yourself again to something you loved doing when it was safe to fail, and before you knew any better. Silence your own censors, those guardians of what is proper and acceptable and logical, and give yourself permission to relax, laugh, and enjoy the page your story is on *right now* without trying to read ahead

the full measure of you

You've been waiting for just the right moment
For everything in your life to feel safer
But if you're gonna write your story
Better put pen to paper
– from "<u>Right Now</u>" by Staci Frenes, Kenon Chen

EARLY ON IN MY CAREER I made my first trip to Nashville in the hopes of catching my big break. I'd recorded a couple of CDs that had garnered some critical attention from a few key people within the Contemporary Christian Music industry, and I'd landed a publishing deal with a small but well-connected publisher. He set up a showcase for me to sing a few of my songs at one of the local clubs on Music Row—12th and Porter. Several record label representatives were invited, and follow-up meetings were scheduled, since my publisher was confident some of the major labels would be interested in sign-ing me to a record deal.

I felt confident, too. I thought I'd paid my share of the proverbial dues—singing in coffeehouses and church youth groups for years, performing in the opening slot for other artists, doing lots of festivals for no money. I felt no hesitancy putting all of my eggs in this one basket, and I figured once the record deal happened, I'd be set. In my mind, getting signed with a major label was the only path to a successful music career that meant I was a "legit" artist, and anything else would not only be an emotional letdown, it would, in essence, prove I wasn't meant to have a career in music.

The good news is I played a great showcase to a packed house that night in Nashville. The bad news is I went to meeting after meeting the following day where I heard variations on these two themes: (1) we've already got a "girl with guitar" on our record label, and (2) since you're with a publisher we're not interested in signing you. (A big part of a record label's revenue comes from publishing royalties on record sales. Almost all record labels own new artists' publishing, or at least a big percentage of it. I didn't know this at the time, and was already with a publisher.)

And that was that. There were no offers. I flew home and for the next six months sank into a deep and ugly depression. I felt like God had tricked me into hoping for something that wasn't going to happen. In my head the whole thing played out like a cruel scenario with God holding my hopes and dreams like a puppeteer and saying to me—*No!*

What I heard in that *no* was that I wasn't talented enough … ready enough … pretty enough … professional enough … and on and on until I came to a place of complete brokenness and confusion. Everything in me was convinced that God had given me the ability to write songs and share them with others. A professional recording career was the only way I could see my dream unfolding, and when it appeared that wasn't going to happen I wanted to be done with it. At the ripe old age of 25 I was ready to throw in the towel.

Remember the Parable of the Talents? One servant buries his talent until the king returns. I know he gets a bad rap as a coward, but I understand him. I *was* him during that season of my life. I felt I'd been told by the music industry that my talent had no worth, and it was powerfully tempting to close off that part of myself and pretend it never happened. I have a feeling that at the root of that servant's cowardice and disobedience was the same fear that wants to grow in each of us with regard to our talent. It's the voice that says, *if I never use my talent, I'll never have to face the awful or surprising truth of whether it's of any value.* For me, the temptation was to think maybe if I just gave up on a music career altogether, I'd never have to risk the pain of disappointment again.

In the months after that Nashville trip I couldn't comprehend the *No*, but I gradually began to understand that both the gift of songwriting and the desire to sing my songs were still with me, even though my dreams didn't materialize in the way I'd wanted them to. I knew in spite of my disappointment and fear of failure I needed to move on with what I'd been created to do. My husband, Abe, and I formed our own record label and publishing company, Stone's Throw Music. We'd learned that the music industry was the metaphorical Goliath to our little David—thus the business names. But we had a few stones in our pocket: the songs I'd written, and a dream to get them heard. I decided to throw myself into the fray of making music as an independent artist, without a record label.

Independent artists must create and find their own outlets for their music, and often those outlets are smaller and more regional than artists with national exposure. Being independent requires doing a lot of your own concert booking and promoting, funding your own recordings, organizing and/or paying for your own radio campaigns, and a lot of other do-it-yourself practices. It's a load of work. But twenty-some years later I haven't regretted the decision to keep making music, even though I *have* had to keep redefining the meaning of "success". I've moved away from what I once thought it was—the big record deal—and closer to the realization that it's simply continuing to do what I love.

Did I really imagine all those years ago that I could just stop writing songs because I didn't get a record deal? Turns out it doesn't work that way. Our gifts are tattooed on our hearts forever. They're non-returnable and they're what bring us our greatest joy and deepest sense of fulfillment. The character I once identified with so closely in the parable—the one who buries his talent—in the end is forced to relinquish it to another and leave the kingdom forever as consequence for his actions. I understand now that when we bury our gifts, we disconnect from our true selves and thus from our Maker. It makes sense that separation from God and from ourselves is what happens when we let fear dictate our choices.

I know a young woman named Jeanette who's about the same age I was when I returned from that Nashville trip—and at a similar crossroads. Jeanette is a dancer. Her entire life has been in preparation for a professional career as a dancer and a choreographer. She's been in dance classes since before she could talk, she trained all through elementary and high school then majored in choreography at a prestigious university. When she graduated she moved to LA, auditioned and got signed to a two-year contract as a dancer on a Disney cruise ship where she was well-paid and able to sharpen her skills with the disciplined routine of two shows a night.

With just a couple of months left on her contract, Jeanette was planning to take her earnings plus a strong recommendation from Disney and move to New York where she'd audition for a spot as a dancer, and eventually work her way up to choreographer with a reputable dance company. What happened instead was an unexpected knee injury during a show that put Jeanette out of commission. She was dropped from her contract and sent home. For the next year specialists and physical therapists tried to determine the exact nature of the injury (a kind of meniscus tear) and how to fix it. Both have been inconclusive, and while she's gradually been getting her strength and flexibility back, she's nowhere near where she was a year ago. According to her doctors, the injury will continue to flare up with strain or overuse indefinitely.

We talked recently, and she was unhappy, restless. She told me it's been forever since she's listened to music and choreographed in her mind—something she did like breathing before the accident. She's facing a tough decision: keep at the slow, painstaking work of training in the hope that she can still land a spot in a dance company, or go back to school for a computer science degree and switch to a different field altogether. She feels the clock ticking on her dance career, and there are no guarantees her body will be ready for the strenuous work of a professional. And yet, dancing and choreographing are all she's ever wanted; they're everything she's worked for and dreamed of since she was a little girl.

I felt my heart breaking for Jeanette, much like it did all those years ago in my own disappointment. I told her a little of my Nashville story, and some of what I learned about myself in the process. I know now that the dreams we have for our talents aren't always the same path we end up on with them, but they're still ours to invest and enjoy. Ultimately I know Jeanette will have to work through the decision of what to do with hers. I hope she'll come to see that there is no burying of her talent without the loneliness of separation from herself and her Maker.

I believe none of us should withhold the full measure of our gifts. In doing so we're depriving ourselves and others of the joy that comes with their use. Like the servants in the parable who invest their talents well, when we do the same we're rewarded with an invitation to *share the joy … which your master enjoys.* (Matthew 25: 23) When we're doing what we're designed to do, no matter what kind of outward success it brings us, we can know it has worth and value, and it brings us pleasure. Much like God himself looked at the work of his hands in Genesis and called it "good." To be invited to share in His joy means, as in so many places throughout Scripture, that God seeks relationship with us. *Enjoy this with me, let's work together,* He seems to be saying. Putting our gifts into practice allows us to experience communion — with God and our true selves.

worth more

The best way to get approval is not to need it.
– Hugh Macleod (cartoonist)

I DID A CONCERT SEVERAL years ago in a city in the Midwest, and when it was over I did my usual routine, heading back to the foyer to stand at my CD table and talk with people who were looking to buy music or just stopping by to say hello. If you've ever done this, sold something you've created — books, jewelry, paintings — *in person*, you know it's an excruciating experience. If you can help it, you get someone else to do it for you. Watching people inspect your work and decide whether or not to buy it is almost unbearably awkward. You have to look away, for your sake and theirs, because you don't want to actually witness (up close and personal) the moment someone decides to walk away and buy nothing. And yet this task is a necessary evil; it's a proven fact that more people tend to buys CDs when I'm actually present at the table than when I'm not. A girl's gotta make a living, so I endure this regular torture with a smile.

Okay, back to the story.

That particular night after my concert a man came up to the merchandise table, glancing around at the CDs I had displayed. When I asked him if there was one song in particular he was looking for, or a certain CD he wanted, he picked one up and announced (a little loudly) that he didn't need to buy a CD since he'd "found this one in the bargain bin for a buck" at his local Christian bookstore a few weeks back. (His exact words in quotes.) It was a supremely awkward moment for everyone within earshot—which was a fair amount of people, given the volume of the pronouncement. I casually tried to laugh it off and congratulated him on finding such a deal, but I was having a completely different internal reaction to his comment.

Initially, I thought it was no big shocker that he'd found a CD of mine somewhere cheaper. I'd been doing this for a few years and once I'd released three or four CDs I started seeing the older titles in the used section at sites like Amazon.com and eBay for as low as forty-nine cents. It's not pretty it's just the reality of the cycle of product life. But there was something particularly awful about hearing someone tell you directly he'd paid a buck for something so personal and hard to place a value on in the first place. I still remember every song on that CD, what was going on in my life when I wrote them, what it cost to make, how hard I worked to get it done, all of that. And here was someone bragging *to my face* that he got it for a buck. Ouch!

I packed up my CDs and the rest of my gear as quickly as I could that night, got into my rental car and sobbed my way back to the hotel where I was staying. In the privacy of my room I had myself an all-out ugly, gut-wrenching bawl fest, and didn't stop until I was puffy, stuffed up and worn out. All sorts of misery and self-pity I didn't know I had inside of me kept churning out tears. I knew it wasn't just about the guy and his rather insensitive bargain bin comment. It was about what his comment had triggered in me. It was about what I thought of myself. He had only given voice to what I most feared: that what I did was basically worthless, and therefore, so was I.

Here's the tricky thing about creating anything: since so much of who we are goes into what we make — the songs we write, the businesses we build, the clothes we sew, the books we write — we naturally derive some, if not a large portion, of our identity from those things. You can't look at a painting by Kandinsky or read a book by Steinbeck and not see traces of the artist in the art. All of the experience and soul and depth of an artist bleeds into their work, so to value the work is also to value the artist who created it. When someone loves my music, I feel in some ways like they love me. They're getting me; they're tracking with my ideas, singing along with my melodies, their hearts are sort of literally and figuratively *in sync* with me. It's a profoundly powerful feeling—having one's work affirmed by others.

Having one's work *de*valued is equally as powerful. That night, crying my eyeballs out over a fairly innocuous comment about finding my CD in a bargain bin revealed a deeper issue I knew I'd wrestle with for a lifetime. On one level I knew my music wasn't literally worth a dollar. In fact, if I really thought about it, it was worth a lot more to me than the ten or fifteen dollar sale price I set. That's just the market value. A random number someone slaps on it can't determine its true value, it can only be felt and known by me, because I created it. No one can begin to understand the nuances and stories behind those songs, the emotional and spiritual ties I have to each one, the slice of life each song represents. How could they? So, whether they buy it for a buck or fifteen dollars, what they pay for it doesn't even come close to the value it holds for me.

But we don't create in our own little worlds just for ourselves. We interact and barter and sell and trade who we are and what we do with the world around us. And though we want desperately to have our work cherished because we feel it's an extension of who we are and the best we have to offer, the reality is not everyone will place the value we do on our work. There are times when we feel demeaned and undervalued by even well-meaning people in our lives, never mind the multitude of Bargain Bin Guys we'll run across. It's inevitable that we will feel used, taken advantage of, misunderstood, and assessed at "face value", and over time, if we take it to heart, our self-worth becomes dangerously eroded.

That's the state I was in that night after the concert. I fell for the lie. I let someone place a value on my creative work — on me — that I feared might actually be true. I'd allowed him — *Bargain Bin Guy, for Pete's sake!* — to determine my worth. It was devastating, but enlightening, because it came with an important realization: I know the stories and life behind the music I write, and therefore its true value. In the same way, *my* Creator knows *me* inside and out. He knows all of my stories, how they began and how they will end. He knows the number of hairs on my head, and has my name written in the palm of His hand. The one who knows me this intimately is the only one who can declare *my* true worth.

I am, according to Ephesians 2:10, *His workmanship created in Christ Jesus for good works. Workmanship* translates differently depending on which Bible version you're reading: *masterpiece, handiwork, creation, the product of His hand, heaven's poetry etched on lives.* Wow. That's you and me. We are His *Mona Lisa*, His Academy-Award winner, His greatest achievement, His most prized and beloved creation. To paraphrase Max Lucado, if God had a wallet, our pictures would be in it. *That's* our true value.

Over the years I've begun to experience the crucial paradigm shift from creating out of a need for an identity defined by others to creating from my true identity as beloved and treasured by God. It's changing many aspects of my creative life, but most especially how I respond to rejection. Getting a *No* from a record company, or a boss at work, or a gallery, or a book publisher doesn't rob us of our identity; it refines it, it chisels and fine-tunes our desire to be our true selves.

Whatever field we're working and creating in, the tug-of-war between defining ourselves by *what we do* rather than *who we are* is a constant challenge. If we believe our work doesn't define our worth, and are secure in that fact, we're free to create for beauty's sake, or for love's sake or for joy's sake, and not because we're looking for something or someone to determine our value. That removes the boundaries, sets us free to do our creative work from an authentic place deeply rooted in our own aesthetic and not one superimposed by the world around us.

Ultimately, Bargain Bin Guy did me a favor. He made me choose how I was going to define my worth: by the slippery, ever-changing opinions of others who don't know me or by the proven words of my Creator who knows me best.

Nobody Loves Me Like You

You were there when my days began
Gave me breath
From the dust formed me with your hand
My heart beat in time with yours
Flesh and bone
I am yours alone
Nobody loves me like you
No one, no one
Nobody loves me like you
Nobody loves me like you
No one, no one
Nobody loves me like you
In the dark and in the brightest light
Only you
See in me a pearl of greatest price
My heart cherished and redeemed
Evermore
I am spoken for
Nobody loves me like you
No one, no one
Nobody loves me like you
Nobody loves me like you
No one, no one
Nobody loves me like you

("Nobody Loves Me Like You" by Staci Frenes © 2012 Stone's
Throw Music/ASCAP)

fearless

To live a creative life
you must lose your fear of being wrong.
– Joseph Chilton Pearce (author)

I MET A WOMAN AT a conference where I was speaking who told me that she used to paint in college almost every day. It was her escape from the endless reading, writing papers, and cramming for tests that college life consisted of. She loved that it brought her much-needed serenity when life got stressful and out of control. Now in her 30's, she was working a nine-to-five job and had become so busy she'd phased out painting from her life altogether. She told me that although she still kept her spare bedroom stocked with paint supplies and an easel, she hadn't touched it in years. I asked her why she let it fall by the wayside for so long. She got choked up trying to articulate her answer, but she realized she deeply regretted it.

What it came down to for my new friend was that during her college years she'd believed she might be good enough to become a full-time artist. But once she'd graduated and started realizing how long it would take her to build enough of a reputation to sell her work for what she needed to live on, she wasn't sure how she'd support herself in the meantime. That and so many other uncertainties about making a living as an artist overwhelmed her and she became discouraged. She convinced herself she didn't have the talent or the drive to sustain a career in art, so she got an office job. Over time it just became easier not to paint at all than to wrestle with old dreams. But that day, as she spilled out her story and her tears, she knew she needed to get back to her painting to feel connected to that place in herself again.

I've talked to dozens of people who recognize their creative gifts but for various reasons have stopped using them. And like my friend at the conference, they almost always regret having given up their piano lessons, or drama class, or the choir they used to sing in. On the surface there are always a handful of pragmatic reasons (time and money being two of the most common) why many of us give up our creative pursuits, but at the root of most of them is some kind of fear. Fear is a creativity killer, and it comes in all shapes and sizes: fear of failure, fear of criticism, fear of our own lack of originality, or lack of discipline to see something through. Fear of success, fear of commitment and fear of change. They all have the same end result: they paralyze us and keep us from taking either the necessary steps to *start* a project or the crucial middle and final steps to *finish* it. Fear cripples our creative muscles, keeping them from movement, action, and the fluid confidence that come from steady use.

One of my favorite books on this topic — *The War of Art* by Steven Pressfield — has helped me battle some of my own fears. That little paperback is dog-eared and underlined from cover to cover. Pressfield addresses what he calls "resistance" in its many forms, with tips and advice on how to overcome it and unblock our creative flow. He contends that we often face the most amount of resistance when approaching the work related to our deepest calling. In other words, we should *expect* opposition when we're doing the very thing we feel most called to do, because the closer we get to who we're created to be, the more our own laziness, fear, apathy and excuses have to get out of the way. Bible teacher, Beth Moore, says it this way, "A person has hardly begun to have a real fight on her hands until she starts serving in her full-throttle giftedness and effectiveness."

My friend Jonah's story is one that left a deep imprint and helps illustrate how fear can paralyze us. He was a shy, quiet kid who didn't socialize much but he took to the guitar quickly, spending hours in his room every day practicing chords and scales. By fourteen he was the lead guitarist in a cover band, playing bars and clubs on the weekends, where he got pulled into the partying lifestyle that went along with it. One weekend when Jonah was 19 years old, though, he went to church with his mom and heard the good news that God loved him and offered him forgiveness — a life free of shame and guilt. He dedicated his heart to serving God and never turned back.

In the months following his decision, Jonah quit the band and got rid of everything that went with it — the drinking and promiscuity, as well as his guitars, amps and CD collection, which he felt were reminders of old ways that needed purging from his life. He got a day job and his own apartment, went to church, joined a young adult Bible study, and for a couple of years immersed himself in this new life. But he felt conflicted. He saw at church how music could encourage and lead people toward God, but didn't know if he could play again without falling into the old self-destructive behavior he associated with it. He was miserable not playing, and torn about whether he should.

One Friday night before falling asleep, Jonah prayed that God would give him specific direction about this conflict. Jonah's mom, who lived nearby and had a key to Jonah's apartment, woke up early that Saturday to go garage-saling (not a word, but it should be). She found a cheap acoustic guitar and thought, *I'll get this for Jonah ... it's been a long time.*

She snuck in and put the guitar on his bed while he was still asleep. When he woke up and saw it, Jonah wept like a baby. He told me he never in a million years imagined God would answer His prayer so tangibly, so personally. It broke his heart, God assuring him that yes, he should do this thing he loved so deeply and brought him so much joy.

Jonah's fear was that he was going to get it wrong—again. He was afraid of his own weakness; afraid of losing himself when he played music. My painter friend from the conference would say her greatest fear was that she'd never accomplish anything of value or worth with her talent. I have friends who have given up on writing a book, playing an instrument, recording an album, showing their work at a gallery—one project after another—because they're afraid the end result will never measure up to their hopes for it. Which is probably the most common and insidious fear of all: the fear of not being all that we want to be, or hope to be.

No wonder Paul speaks such powerful words to his young friend Timothy about fear, and how it relates to his gift: *I'm reminding you to revive God's gift that is in you … God didn't give us a spirit of fear, but one of power and of love and a sound mind.* (2 Timothy 1: 6-7) Paul had prayed over Timothy and encouraged him to use his gift of teaching the way he'd seen and learned from Paul himself. Although Timothy was young, Paul saw in him great promise, and reminded him of this many times in his letters when Timothy struggled, feeling overwhelmed, inexperienced, and intimidated by those who professed to be more experienced and knowledgeable.

I can relate to Timothy. Especially when I was first starting to play shows as a young singer/songwriter, but even now when I have doubts about my ability. I question my level of talent compared with other more successful, experienced artists who have more awards and accolades under their belts. I wonder who would ever want to listen to me. What do I have to say that's any different from what's already been said? My natural tendency is to play it safe and *do nothing,* because at least then I won't risk rejection, disappointment, or failure. That particular wrestling match is a familiar one that can cripple me for days, weeks, even months at a time.

It's exactly why these two verses in 2 Timothy are so invaluable and heartening. They remind me that along with my gifts, God has actually given me everything I need to use them *boldly, sensibly,* and *lovingly.* When I take this truth fully to heart, letting it seep into the marrow of my self-doubt where I've allowed fear of failure and inadequacies to reign, I *do* experience a revival, a rekindling of the flame that was first lit in me as a child. If fear is the greatest sabotage to our creative lives, keeping us in the darkness of intimidation and paralysis, then surely *power, love,* and *a sound mind* are our best defenses against it.

Discipline (a sound mind) and authority (power) allow us to navigate wisely and administrate keenly the opportunities our gift opens up for us. When our motive is to serve others in love, failure and success are irrelevant. Feelings of intimidation disappear, because we're not competing or comparing, we're offering our gifts to enrich the world and others, not advance ourselves. *Perfect love casts out fear.* (1 John 4:18) Our creative work thrives in the absence of fear. It can be done without the need for approval, without the expectation of getting something in return.

Fear is a thief; it attempts to rob us of every good thing that's ours. But God in His boundless love continues to replenish and equip us in every area we're lacking.

The Thief and the Lover

This is how you know the thief's been here
By the things you start to notice disappear
You open up and reach inside your heart
Everything is empty and dark
All the good is gone
You laugh less, you thank less
You risk less than before
You have less so you give less
You love less and it shows
That's how you'll know

The lover comes to bring back what is yours
All that was stolen and so much more
From a well so deep you drink it in
'Til your thirsty heart is filled again
And it overflows
You laugh more, you thank more
You risk more than before
You have more, so you give more
You love more and it shows
That's how you know
Make no mistake the thief will come
Don't let him undo what love has done

("The Thief and the Lover" by Staci Frenes © 2012 Stone's Throw
Music/ASCAP)

creative identity: gather your seeds

Reader Reflection Questions

Do you see your creativity as something that's compartmentalized into certain activities, or do you find that creating, in some fashion, is integral to your everyday life?

What are the particular talents you've been given that are suited to your personality and strengths? Do you recognize these as gifts of worth and value, or do you find that you downplay and undervalue them?

Was there a time in your life when 'playing' in your area of creativity helped to develop and nurture it? Do you find that you still give yourself time for that, or is it pushed aside by the more pragmatic demands of your life?

Just for fun, take a minute to daydream about your wildest hopes for your own area of creativity. What would you absolutely LOVE to be doing with your writing, sewing, painting, web design, etc? What would that look like, feel like?

Reflect on a time when someone's rejection of you, or

your work, sunk in deeper than you expected. Revisit that experience with the understanding of your true worth in Jesus Christ that Ephesians 2:10 promises. Marinate in it and let it ease the sting you still feel from that wound.

In The War of Art Steven Pressfield contends that we often face the most amount of resistance when approaching the work related to our deepest calling. Evangelical Bible teacher, Beth Moore, says, "A person has hardly begun to have a real fight on her hands until she starts serving in her full-throttle giftedness and effectiveness."

Does this concept resonate with you? If there's resistance or fight when you're doing the things you feel are at the core of what you're 'called' to do, how does it manifest itself?

creative practices:
cultivate your fields

breathe in

...the essential is still deeply embedded in mystery.
It is not answerable
to any of our formulas.
– Flannery O'Connor (author)

SOMEDAY I'D LIKE TO VISIT St. Paul's Cathedral in London. Apparently it features one of the best examples of the acoustic phenomenon known as a *whispering gallery*. The cathedral's huge dome sits high above an intersection of four segments, which is where worshippers gather underneath regularly for mass. If you climb the 250 stairs or so you reach a platform that runs all the way around the interior of the dome. Anywhere along that walkway if you turn and whisper into one side of the dome, the sound skims around the inside, and your friend can hear it just as loudly on the other side—some 30 to 35 feet away. People have said it sounds like the whisper is emerging from the wall. Fascinating. I could have some fun in this place. Imagine whispering nonsense things to people across the room who have no idea where it's coming from.

I see a metaphor in the whispering gallery for the human heart: a curved chamber built for worship, intricately and exquisitely tuned to hear even the faintest whisper. The whisperer is *the still small voice* within, whispering words of inspiration, comfort, hope, or strength that reach us with startling clarity. Historians say the whispering gallery was pure accident—the architects had no idea sound waves would hug the walls of the dome and travel such distances without weakening. But we're designed to know and be known intimately by our Creator; to hear His voice whisper inside the sacred chamber of our hearts. That whisper is our inspiration, our muse, our connection to what writer Flannery O'Connor calls "the essential ... deeply embedded in mystery."

I've heard artists of all kinds—actors, musicians, novelists, painters—from various religious persuasions say their greatest work comes from a source outside of themselves. That the moments of most profound inspiration were not strokes of genius they could explain and take credit for, but mysterious breakthroughs where they'd felt like they were channeling a force bigger and more complex than anything they could manage. Some say it's as though the poem, song, or book they wrote already existed in some other realm and needed to be received. Many artists see the creative process as the challenge to hear what's being spoken in its purest form—like the whisper across the dome of St. Paul's Cathedral—then to translate that through their art. Maybe inspiration—that one percent magic or mystery, that inexplicable moment the light bulb turns on or the waterfall rushes in—isn't and can't ever be something we ourselves manufacture. Maybe it, in fact, comes from a source inside of us but beyond our understanding.

The ancient Greek poet, Homer, claimed it was the Muses that inspired not only his works, *The Odyssey* and *The Iliad,* but all poetry, music, dance, theater, and astronomy. If an artist lacked inspiration, the ancient Greeks believed he should pray to the Muse associated with his creative genius, and she would visit him in the night, whispering a tune or an idea into his ear. The notion of the muse, even in modern references, (*Eat Pray Love*'s Liz Gilbert's TED talk is one of my favorites) is a fairly common one. It suggests that the artist is not alone when she creates; someone is present, helping to stir the creative pot.

It makes sense, then, that when we talk about cultivating a creative life we are talking about staying deeply connected to the Spirit as the source of our inspiration. That connection, according to this passage in Corinthians, gives us access to the deepest mysteries there are: the very thoughts of God Himself.

...the Spirit searches everything, even the depths of God. No one comprehends the thoughts of God except the Spirit of God ... Now we have received not the spirit of the world, but the Spirit who is from God, that we might understand the things freely given us by God.
(1 Corinthians 2:11-13)

I've known song ideas to come from every source imaginable: a conversation, a movie scene, a passage in a book, a look in someone's eye, a phrase, a walk, a drive, a photograph. Those are the triggers that stir something deeper in my heart—more of a feeling than a single word or a particular melody. It's usually an emotion or a truth so honest and raw that at first it's hard to even articulate, like *a lump in the throat*, to borrow a phrase from Robert Frost. I've come to understand that those are inspired moments, when something eternal gets whispered to me from across the dome of my heart from my Muse—the Holy Spirit. The ideas that come from those moments I treat like exquisite gifts. I explore and develop them carefully and thoroughly because I know at their core is something true, something worth saying well and artfully. Sometimes I get it right, sometimes I just keep chasing it.

If we're honest, those of us that do any kind of creative work will admit that not all of it is inspired; but I dare say our best work is. It has a transcendent quality, it evokes something more than what's seen or experienced on the surface. The word *inspired* literally means *filled with spirit*. The origin of *spirit* is the Latin word, *spiritus,* meaning *breath.* In Genesis 1:26 God says, *Let us make man in our image*. He forms man from the dust of the ground then breathes His breath—His Spirit, His life-force—into the nostrils of Adam, and what was dust becomes flesh and blood. Without breath, there is no essence—soul, personality, being—inside the shape and form of Adam. Job 33:4 echoes this: *The spirit of God has made me, and the breath of the Almighty gives me life.*

The same is true of the work we create. Without the inspiration of God to give it life it's only dust and clay, no matter how beautiful it may look to the world. I've written songs like that; too many to count over the years, in fact. Songs I haven't felt personally invested in. Songs that, looking back on them now, have no meaning or personal value to me beyond serving a finite purpose in the moment. They're not any less skillfully written, there's just no breath of anything true or meaningful in them.

When we're naturally gifted in a certain area, it's easy to switch into autopilot—to make a living, to meet a deadline, to keep our skills sharpened, or even as a survival mode, because we're depleted and just need to rest. Whereas staying present involves being actively engaged in listening, seeking, meditating, and hearing what the Spirit is saying. Those things take time and discipline, and if we're not doing them regularly we can easily start churning out cookie-cutter work that might pass for authentic to some, but that we know has no life in it.

What profit is the image, that its maker should carve it …
yet in it there is no breath at all.
(Habakkuk 2:18-19)

As artists and people in whom God has placed His own Spirit, our highest calling is to write, sing, draw, and make what we hear Him speak into our hearts. We are conduits of creative work that contain eternal, lasting truths. In our prayers and cries for direction, reading His word, meditating on its meaning and implications, God's still small voice invites us into the mysteries of a world we don't fully understand.

Life brings with it a steady flow of distracting static, interrupting and distorting our receptivity. To create work that reflects the depth and beauty of that mystery, we need to fine-tune our hearts to hear Him whisper—like twisting a sensitive radio knob ever so slightly to pick up the clearest possible signal. My heart longs to hear and know only the voice of God in the midst of a noisy world. If I'm assured of that one thing—that it's His voice I'm hearing and not another's—I am confident to move or stay where He tells me in my creative life.

Know Your Voice

Whispers and echoes
Down a long dark hallway
Don't know where one begins
Where another fades away
So many different voices
Fight for my attention
It's overwhelming and it's making me feel afraid
Afraid I'll miss the sound
Your tender love makes
I wanna tune you in every time you say my name
I want to know your voice
Every time I hear you callin'
Help me to know your voice
I won't be afraid to follow
If I know it's you
If I know it's you
Into the darkness
Into the deep
Into the promise of a new day
If it's where you lead
I will follow, I will follow
If I know it's you

find your flow

*There is a vitality, a life force, a quickening that is
translated through you into action,
and because there is only one of you in all time, this
expression is unique.
If you block it, it will never exist through any other
medium and be lost.*
– Martha Graham (choreographer)

LEONARD COHEN, THE GREAT AMERICAN
songwriter of "Hallelujah" and other songs, was
asked once in an interview why he writes mostly
melancholy, moody songs as opposed to upbeat, op-
timistic tunes. He explained that for many years he
lamented that phenomena in his career, and he
would often ask himself the same thing when he sat
down at the piano intending to write something
happy and life-affirming like, "What A Wonderful
World" by Louis Armstrong, a song for which he had
great admiration. Cohen said once he got into a creative mindset where the ideas started to come and the
melodies and chords began taking shape, he was

compelled to "go where the flow of energy" took him, and not try to change its direction. When he followed that, he said, it usually took him down the dark roads to minor chords and slower tempos.

Cohen learned over and over again that as much as he liked the idea of writing a happy song, he found that he just couldn't do it. He had to follow the musical ideas that felt most comfortable, authentic, and ultimately most pleasurable for him to write. He recognized that for him to write a song outside of that vein would have felt forced, artificial, and unnatural. After many years of fighting it he finally stopped trying to change that about himself, he said. Instead, he surrendered to what came from his own flow of ideas and energy, not what came from a siphoned trickle he'd once tried to force from somewhere outside of himself.

In your area of creativity, chances are if you're following your own natural flow you're going to be fulfilled, content, and even happy. Sometimes, as in Cohen's songwriting, you find where you're most comfortable by trying to go somewhere else first. Those tangential explorations into unfamiliar waters are necessary for showing us what we can do — grow, stretch, diversify — but also for showing us where we just plain don't belong. That was true in my case. Discovering what I really loved and wanted to do with my life involved paying attention to what I *shouldn't* be doing, and learning from that.

When I was in college I wrestled with what my major should be. I declared Music my freshman year, but as a songwriter my approach had always been more intuitive than trained, so studying it in school didn't feel like a good fit. Plus, I'd had "the talk" about my future with my dad before going into college and it steered my thinking in a more practical direction. He pointed out that I could always change my major to my other love—English—and teach school while pursuing music on the side. I couldn't refute that logic, so at the beginning of my junior year I started on that path.

Once I graduated and got my first teaching job, though, I saw that it was going to take some serious juggling of my time and energy to continue to write, record, and perform music while holding down a full-time position. I taught for several years and recorded four album projects before eventually switching to part-time status as a teacher. And the truth is, by that time I was miserable. I woke up most days feeling depressed, depleted, and drained. Teaching felt like an almost physical tearing away from my true love, music. I'd scribble song lyrics on scraps of paper during breaks, and try to sing ideas into a voice recorder on the commute to and from school, but I felt so divided and pulled by the end of the day I'd come home in tears.

Looking back on it now, although I felt like I needed to hang on to the job for financial reasons, I think I was being nudged to make the leap toward full-time music a lot sooner than I actually did it. I had no passion or energy for teaching and the longer I stayed in it the more drained and tapped out I became. Songwriting, on the other hand, always energized me and put fuel in my emotional tank—even when it physically exhausted me. I think in my attempt to be practical and responsible, I ignored the nagging reality that I wasn't experiencing peace or joy in my job. I held onto it because of my fear of change, fear of the unknown, fear of not making enough money to pay the bills. But when I finally let go of it to pursue music full-time, I felt the weight of that fear and dread slide off of me like a heavy coat.

When we recognize and understand what unique personality traits, talents and passions are knit into our deepest fibers, pursuing opportunities and experiences where those are most actively engaged will bring us our greatest joy. Those conflicted years were some of the hardest I've experienced in my creative life. I learned a valuable lesson at the high cost of my own peace and well being: if I'm doing something that consistently makes me stressed, depleted, anxious, and burned out, and feeling far from myself and God, chances are I shouldn't be doing it. I'm either in it for the wrong reasons, or more likely, I'm simply not doing what I love.

My younger sister, Heidi, found her creative path as differently from me as our personalities are.

As a kid, she had no real love for the poems and songs that brought me such joy. In fact, to this day she reminds me of the torment I put her through when I forced her to sing duets with me at family Christmas gatherings or made her play parts in the plays and musicals I wrote. (Sorry, Heidi, I was just following my creative flow ... plus, I was older and bossier, so you had no chance against me.)

Instead, Heidi was happiest when experimenting with the latest techie gadgets and gizmos she could get her hands on. Before there were cell phones, digital cameras, or mp3 players, and before everyone had home computers (gasp!) Heidi loved tinkering with Polaroid cameras, transistor radios, remote control toys, battery operated microphones and any other mechanical doodad of the day. Especially anything camera equipment-related; that was her favorite. While my strongest memories of visits to my grandparents' house involved spending time watching my Nana sew, Heidi's most vivid memories were of watching home movies and slide shows on my grandpa's portable pull-up projector screen. What fascinated her, she says, was how the pictures on the screen could tell stories without words.

Heidi was drawn to visual media long before she knew what it was or that it had a name. In college she floundered around in different majors, eventually landing on Communications—but even that seemed too generic for what she wanted to do, which although she couldn't articulate it at the time, was to combine her love of technology and her love of story-telling through images. She traveled for a while, eventually moving to Nashville in her early twenties, working odd jobs here and there for friends in the music industry. And when the 80's ushered in video technology and MTV exploded onto the music scene, Heidi found her calling in video production.

Some of Heidi's most fulfilling work has involved traveling overseas with organizations like World Vision to shoot footage of children in remote locations like the rural villages in Lesotho, Africa, playing, working, and often barely surviving. She edits the footage to create short, poignant stories that are shared with audiences all over the country—in stadiums and event centers and churches—in efforts to raise awareness for the desperate needs of the world's poorest children. I continue to be amazed at the level of excellence in her work, which is in constant demand by some of the top names in Nash-ville's music scene. I'm thrilled to have collaborated on one of these videos with Heidi with my songs, "Dreaming Us". It's one of my all time favorite videos she's done.

Now, after several years with her own successful video production company—Cinemation Media—under her belt, Heidi and I talk about how our early tendencies and sensibilities sometimes lead us in circuitous routes before reaching the destination we're meant to find. Because her specific area of expertise, digital video editing, wasn't showing up in any college catalogues or job listings when she was trying to decide what to do with her life, she wasn't always sure which way to turn. But in hindsight, she can see early indicators that she was following her instincts, her passion; and those eventually led her to the uncharted opportunities in a field she finds incredibly rewarding.

Follow your flow—the things you love and the things you're good at. It will lead you into those opportunities that most utilize and engage your strengths and passions. Trust that your personality and talents uniquely equip you for what's uniquely yours to do.

do what you love

Let the beauty we love be what we do.
– Rumi (poet)

IN LUCY SHAW'S BOOK, *Breath for the Bones*, she tells of an 18th century housewife living on the Canadian prairie. In one of her journal entries this housewife writes about surviving the sub-zero winter temperatures by making quilts for her family. She writes, "I make them warm to keep my family from freezing; I make them beautiful to keep my heart from breaking." Finding what it is that we need to do to keep our hearts from breaking, to maintain our sanity and well-being in a world full of challenges, stress and pain is no small or inconsequential feat.

I've always found it fascinating that we each lean toward an aesthetic that's uniquely our own. We love what we love. Most of us were (or are) attracted to a *type* when we date. We like certain color schemes , movie genres, musical styles. We gravitate toward a certain kind of art or flavor of foods over others. We know when something we wear just feels *right,* and when something doesn't. It's true of how we like to spend our time, too. I'm thrilled when I can wander around a bookstore for hours, but some of my friends would much rather go clothes shopping (the well-dressed ones), or antique hunting (the ones with cool houses) or hiking (the tan, fit ones). We love what we love; which in part explains why we follow certain creative paths over others.

My friend Alison has been sewing and creating with fabric for decades. She enjoys every step of the creative process, and for as long as I've known her, she's always somewhere in the middle of designing or making something—pillows, aprons, table linens, and baby quilts, to name just a few. Usually, her projects are gifts for others. I know for a fact that Alison stays creatively busy because for her, nothing beats knowing the happiness someone feels when they receive one of her handcrafted pieces. "My heart soars each time," she says. (Have I mentioned what a lovely human being Alison is?)

Beyond just the sheer joy that comes from making new things and sharing them with friends and family, this creative passion has been extremely important and even necessary in Alison's life, especially when dealing with the sudden death of her husband a few years ago. His passing shook and changed her entire world. She not only lost the love of her life, her best friend, and the father of her children, she lost herself for a good while. She experienced that painful reality that so many understand when losing a life-long partner: when you truly build your life around someone for 30 years, it's difficult to suddenly be on your own.

But Alison's passion for creating came to her emotional rescue. To cope with the new life she was unexpectedly forced to live, she leaned on her love for sewing and making things to boost her spirits, energize her, and crawl out of depression. She helped out with a friend's sewing business for a while, and then started her own, Material Impressions, LLC, which she dedicated to her late husband—her biggest fan and cheerleader. He'd often exclaim that he was going to give up his law practice and help her pursue her handcrafting business. His faith sowed a seed in her heart. Now, a few short years after the darkest season in her life, Alison wrote in an email recently, "God is good! This artistic talent is His gift to me and I will continue to nurture it and with it, hopefully, bring beauty and joy to others; a blessed cycle indeed."

Last year I read Gretchen Rubin's book, *The Happiness Project*, thinking it might inspire me and help me deal with some of my sadness after my dad passed away. She discusses several practices that, according to her research, are shown to boost one's happiness. One of the foundational concepts she discovered in the research, and again when applying it to her own life, is something she calls *Do what you do.*

She cites specific examples in her own life and in the cases she studies, then boils the concept down to a simple truth: the more we try to please others, or follow societal or self-imposed rules or standards of "happiness", the more disconnected we feel from our true selves, and thus our sense of well-being. As we come to understand more intimately how we're wired and what we're good at, and then invest our time and energy doing *those* things, the happier we are.

A dear friend of mine, Taya, has lived in a tiny town in the Midwest for over 20 years, moving there from the West Coast to get married, have a family and eventually homeschool three boys while her husband's career kept him on the road for long periods at a time. One of Taya's gifts is cooking; in fact, she's more of a chef than a cook. She makes exotic, delicious dishes on a daily basis, complete with home-grown herbs and fresh local ingredients. Her meals look like they're straight out of *Bon Appétit*. I know this because Taya posts beautiful drool-worthy photos of her meals for the rest of us slackers on Instagram and Facebook. It never fails, on a night I've fed my family hot dogs and boxed mac-n-cheese for dinner, Taya will post a photo of what *she* made, and a description that reads something like, *Pancetta crisps with goat cheese and figs, basil cucumber salad with goat cheese and pecans, and a raspberry mascarpone-creme tart for dessert.* (No kidding, that's an actual meal she made. On a week night. For three boys!)

Lucky for me, I've eaten in Taya's home many times and can testify that her food tastes as good as it looks. I'm always amazed at the attention to detail in her cooking as well as her presentation—which is something I've learned *real* cooks care about. Her taste and sense of beauty are evident in her fabulous meals and also in her signature handcrafted cocktails, another plus of dining at Taya's. I believe preparing gourmet meals for others fulfills her and nourishes her like her own wonderful food nourishes those of us who eat it. She's an artist who finds her energy and creative flow, and perhaps even a measure of reprieve from the loneliness of small town life, in creating beautiful and tasty food.

I wonder how many of us know what keeps our hearts from breaking. Like Alison working through her grief, when we experience pain or disappointment or loss can we find comfort in doing an activity related to our creativity? When we're stressed with obligations, deadlines, financial pressure, do we recognize what we need to do to unplug and escape into our own imaginations? And when we're numb from getting battered by one season of trouble after another, do we know how to stir up those creative embers and feel the warmth of our own deep joy again?

Not long ago, I found myself in one of those seasons—a long, dry spell during which my family and I were going through some of the most painful struggles we'd ever experienced together. We had lost our home in the housing market crash in California, and with it my husband's job (also in the financial industry) took a huge nosedive. Our son was going through some intense mental health issues that left us searching for answers from psychiatrists, hospitals and faith-based counselors. My dad was diagnosed with stage IV lung cancer. Financially, spiritually, emotionally — in almost every area we could get knocked down, we were getting hit. I found myself not wanting to feel anything anymore. It hurt too much, so I pushed it all down where I wouldn't let myself access it. I hadn't written any songs in over a year because songwriting would take me where I didn't want to go — way down deep to the source of my pain, and I couldn't bear to dig around in that wreckage.

I don't know why then, one day near the end of that season, I picked up my guitar and started strumming a few chords in search of a melody or a lyric. But I did, and as I played, I felt something like liquid seep in and soften the places that had become hard. Like sunlight, lighting the dark corners of my despair. I wrote a song that day, and it helped open up the sealed tomb of pain and started the process of bringing me back to life. It helped me to feel and eventually hope and pray and dream again. It kept my heart from breaking, because like the prairie housewife with her quilt, I needed to create something beautiful where I could see no beauty.

Genesis tells us that when He finished creating the heavens and the earth, "God saw that it was good," and I wept while I was writing most of that song. I wept for joy, because I saw that it was good. Good for me — it was the ax breaking the frozen sea inside of me, as Kafka says art does. And I hoped it would be good for others, too, who felt numb, paralyzed, dead in their own pain.

This is the song that came to me that day — like the hope of Emily Dickinson's poem, it was a bird that flew down and perched on my soul.

Everything You Love Comes Alive

Your love is liquid
Filling the hollow places
With warmth and weight
Changing the landscape
Rivers melting through my
Frozen veins
Everything is stirring inside
Everything you love comes alive
And I'm alive
I'm alive

("Everything You Love Comes Alive" by Staci Frenes © 2012
Stone's Throw Music/ASCAP)

pay attention

Glance is the enemy of vision.
– Ezra Pound (poet)

ONE AFTERNOON I DROVE WITH my band several hours outside of the San Francisco Bay Area where I live to the Sierra Nevada foothills where we were going to play music for a church the following morning. The plan was to stay at the home of a family that had offered us overnight accommodations while they were away on vacation. We followed our directions, getting off the main highway and taking a series of twisting roads that led us farther and farther away from signs of civilization. We finally reached a remote dirt trail that led, winding and narrow, to a dead end. It was pitch black, and we city folk had a rough time finding the house nestled far back from the road in a line of trees that clustered along a mountain ridge.

But oh, was it ever worth finding. The house was magnificent. It was a two-story Victorian-style manor with a wraparound porch and lush gardens on all sides. We wandered quietly through room after room before we finally sank into the Adirondack chairs on the back porch that overlooked a vast ravine of treetops and distant mountain peaks. But the real view was right over our heads: it was the most brilliant and dense expanse of stars I've ever seen on one of the clearest nights I can remember in years. It was spectacular.

The longer we looked up, the more our eyes grew accustomed to the darkness and the stars seemed to multiply. The Milky Way looked like handfuls of glitter tossed across black velvet. From different directions, stars shot across the sky in perfect arcs, leaving chalky-white trails that lasted a few seconds before burning out. We kept trying to point them out to each other, oohing and ahhing, feeling like the VIP audience to a private showing of some cosmic light parade. If ever there was a time I felt David's words in the Psalms, it was that night: *The heavens declare the glory of God; and the sky above proclaims his handiwork.* It was undeniable and glorious, His fingerprints across the sky. We felt giddy and privileged, the children of a generous Father who delights in doing wondrous things for us.

That experience stayed with me for weeks. Back home in the city I kept wondering why the night sky looked so full of light and movement up in the mountains, when I couldn't see it from my own house. I read somewhere that "light pollution" (the astronomers call it) from street lamps, cars, houses, and nearby shops obscures the true view of the sky. It wasn't that the sky itself had changed; my perspective had. My vision was clouded with the lesser light of my surroundings. I realized—and was astonished by—how much *life* there is in the sky at night. Life that goes largely unnoticed. I'm grateful I was out on that porch, lifting my head up and taking it all in. Times like those are precious and inspiring not only in my spiritual life, but in my creative life, too. The song, "Meteor Shower" came from that experience— it was fertile with beauty and meaning for me.

Meteor Shower

Under your silent sky I am keeping watch
For signs of life from the world beyond
Where waves stand still and mountains move
With just a word from you
I wish for a glimpse tonight, a falling star
Arrows of flaming light to tear apart
This veil between the earth and sky
Illuminate the night
Like a meteor shower fall on me
Revealer of wonders wash over me
Break through my atmosphere
Leave a million traces here in my heart
Like a meteor shower

flourish

A meteor shower

("Meteor Shower" by Staci Frenes, Nate Sabin © 2008 Stone's Throw Music/ASCAP Lorilu music/ASCAP)

The shooting stars we saw that night were unexpected reminders that the sky holds much more than what we see most of the time. Proof that when we pay attention, slow down, remove ourselves from distractions—or the distractions from us—and focus on the sky above or the world around, we are often rewarded with delightful, rare sightings of beauty. In one of my favorite movies, *Stranger Than Fiction,* Will Farrell's character says, "It's the anomalies that save us." In other words, it's the unannounced interruptions breaking through the skin of our mundane lives that remind us there's more going on in the universe than what appears at first glance. It often takes a second or third or more prolonged look for us to notice what others don't.

An observant eye catches even the fleeting glimpses of beauty, and it's those glimpses, like the one I had of the meteor shower, that afford us a wealth of ideas and inspiration for the creative work we do. As a musician, I was moved by that meteor shower experience to write a song. Maybe if I'd had any kind of painting skills I could have painted that sky like Van Gogh did. My math teacher friend, Stephanie might have created a lesson plan about how to calculate the vast distance between stars and use it as an illustration in class the next day. My friend, Jill, who writes children's books, might have written a story about those shooting stars, giving them names and personalities. Which, on second thought, may have turned out to be more of a horror story—seeing as how they plunged to their death. Ok, so I'm not a children's writer, but you get the idea.

In any creative field, new ideas are the fodder that feeds our work. Without them, what we do starts to become stale, a rehash of what's already being done. Insight and revelation that lead to fresh and interesting ideas are often the result of happy accidents, anomalies ... unexpected meteor showers from heaven. We don't lack for material—it's all here. We shape our works of art from the clay right under our feet. Conversations with friends, places we visit, movies we see, books we read, a line in a song, the way birds gather and swoop in one graceful motion. When we stay open, receptive, and take in everything through all of our senses, something we notice will catch our attention, illuminate our imagination or sink to the pit of our stomach. We need to trust these out-of-the-ordinary reactions to ordinary encounters. It means our life is speaking and we're listening.

There's a verse in Isaiah that reminds me to keep my ears and eyes tuned for surprises, new sources of inspiration for songs, new directions to follow in my creativity: *Behold I will do something new, now it will spring forth. Will you not see it? I will make a roadway in the wilderness, rivers in the desert ... Will you not see it?* (43:19) I see in these lines an almost urgent directive—*will you not see it?*—to pay attention, to not just *look* but also actually see the new thing God is doing. And whatever *it* is, it's going to be provision or refreshment you hadn't thought would be there— a path through the wilderness, a stream in a desert.

It may be a surprising moment of refreshment, or guidance, or clarity in the middle of a mental fog. And often you'll find in it a new solution to something that's been bothering you, giving you enough of a fresh perspective on a dormant project to allow you to move forward. Like one of those Rorschach tests: one minute you're seeing a messy blob of ink on the page and the next minute you're seeing the outline of two faces looking at each other. You may be looking for a long time at a roadblock that seems impossible, unfixable, a dead-end. And without warning, you discover that you have new eyes for it. You can make out a pathway through it, or provision in it.

I'm a walker. My body wasn't built for running, or at least that's my story and I'm sticking to it. When I run I don't hear from God, I hear from my aching feet and pounding head. But when I walk, I can focus and *behold.* It's not always as easy as it sounds. I walk the same route most of the time, and it can get old, familiar … and I can easily cease to see anything new in it. But sometimes I turn down the noise of distraction and start noticing things I hadn't before. I start to really see newness even in the familiar. When I do that, when my heart and my mind are open and tuned in, the mystery and beauty of God's presence show up all over the place, and the world around becomes the love language by which the Creator woos me.

That's How You Woo Me

Every sunrise speaks your promise
Evening your faithfulness
The starry sky writes your love letter
Beauty my heart can't miss
One word, one touch
One pulse at a time
That's how you woo me
Chasing my heart
One beat at a time
That's how you woo me
Every soft wind breathes your whisper
Every smile your kiss
Your presence in the dark so tender
Calling my heart to rest
I can't count the ways
You orchestrate every little thing

flourish

Just to say you love me
Pursuing me relentlessly
Every soft rain brings your mercy
Showers me like a gift
Every love songs tells our story
How can my heart resist

("That's How You Woo Me" by Staci Frenes © 2012 Stone's
Throw Music/ASCAP)

focus your lens

I have no special talents.
I am only passionately curious.
– Albert Einstein (scientist, inventor)

I LOVE THE DOCUMENTARY, *Man on Wire,* based
on the book by Philippe Petit, a high-wire artist who
walked along a tightrope 1,300 feet in the air between
the Twin Towers of the World Trade Center in 1974
while stunned New Yorkers watched below. Film-
maker James Marsh read Petit's book years later and
felt the story immediately pull him in. His curiosity
led him to pursue the making of the film, which won
an Academy Award. Marsh said in an interview,
"Curiosity is a big, big part of what I do ... it's an in-
stinctive reaction to something that excites me and
immediately begins to stimulate other thoughts, other ideas, images, insights." Watching the black and
white documentary, which consists of flashbacks,
interviews, old photographs and rare footage, I saw
this fascinating story unfold through the lens of
Marsh's curious perspective, and found it mesmeriz-

ing.

Author Seth Godin (*Purple Cow*) says our job as creative people is to *wonder at something no one else is wondering about*, and then invite others to wonder with us through our art. Like Marsh with his documentary, what we're curious about becomes the unique focus of our creative work, and helps give it a distinct identity. We might all be watching the same thing, but we're not all having the same experience because we're watching from different perspectives, literally through different eyes. And although the world itself isn't new—our great-great-great-grandparents looked at the same sun, moon and stars; breathed the same air, walked the same earth as we do—what *is* new is your heart and brain processing what you see, filtering it and then interpreting it in a way that's unique to you.

What do you wonder at? What makes you curious? What rabbit trails or tangents do you find yourself following? The Internet is our age's virtual library of endless information—there's not a single interest that can't be explored online. Track your movement every once in a while by checking your browser's history, just to see patterns in what can sometimes feel like random trips through the web. That'll give you a hint of what you're curious about. Based on a completely random and unofficial poll among a few friends of mine, the most common interests based on web searches seem to be travel, books, cooking, technology, music and fashion. Mine included a handful of sites related to poetry, music marketing, and creativity. (And maybe an occasional cocktail recipe or two. Give or take.)

When you're following your curiosity toward those things that pique your interest and hold your attention, you'll often find in them the inspiration and materials for your creativity. Growing up, I remember my parents loved to spend their weekends foraging through antique stores, junkyards and garage sales for old furniture pieces they could strip, stain, or cover in fabric or paint for our home or garden. Eclectic. Refurbished. Vintage. My parents were into cool decor before it even had a name. To this day I have vivid memories of some of those repurposed pieces in some of our old homes. A rusty birdcage stripped and repainted distressed yellow hung in the sunroom. A battered-up door stripped, then restained (to look even more beat up) with a funky new doorknob sat propped up in the garden. And an antique Radio Flyer kids' wagon filled with potting soil and flowers decorated the front porch. The more out of context the piece was from its surroundings, the more it seemed to stand out and create an artistic statement, making us see it with new eyes.

The things we're curious about and then find a way to share in our area of creativity can illuminate corners of the world others might not normally see. I learn something new all the time observing some of my photographer friends' work. The best photos seem to find something striking in the obscure, hidden places: a candid expression on an elderly shopkeeper's face, a thin shaft of light through a cluster of trees, a rare flower on the cusp of blooming. Looking at these shots, I get the benefit of being behind someone else's lens seeing through their filters.

Good fiction writers, in a similar way, are naturally perceptive and intuitive people. They watch, they listen, they notice subtle expression changes, body language, vocal intonations. They're sensitive to human nature in ways that help them craft better stories and write believable characters. I love a well-written book more than I love chocolate or the beach—high praise!—because it takes me to worlds I never knew existed, both inside the psyche and exotic locations I'll probably never visit.

Cultivating creativity involves trusting your instincts and point of view, not in spite of the fact that they're yours and no one else has them, but because of it. Your perspective is your personality—your art. How you saw the building blocks in the sandbox as a kid may later show up in how you arrange flowers in your business as a florist. If your creativity looks different, sounds different, tastes different and feels different than anyone else's, you've created a distinct imprint. Your confidence in the unique quirks and even imperfections of that imprint is crucial to you doing your best authentic work.

One of my favorite people and best friends, Lori, used to host an event called "Funky Barn" in the big red barn on her property in Minnesota. Vendors set up booths for the weekend and sold their handcraft-ed wares—jewelry, paintings, baby clothing, knit-wear, home decor pieces, and a lot more. It was a popular event for which artists often reserved space months ahead of time. Lori made jewelry and mixed media art and had a good eye for quality work, so she screened the potential vendors for each Funky Barn event. If certain applicants weren't quite up to par she had the unlucky job of turning them down. She hated doing this. Lori is the sweetest, kindest person on the planet, and it pained her to hurt any-one's feelings. Every once in a while she'd ask me for a second opinion about a potential vendor's work, e-mailing me a few pictures or a website link. I knew she trusted me to give her my honest opinion, and I had no trouble doing that.

One weekend when I was traveling and had a long layover at the Phoenix airport, Lori texted to ask if I had time to take a look at some jewelry pieces and tell her what I thought. I signed into Gmail so we were able to message back and forth while she sent me the pics. Each one showed a different necklace worn by a woman in a pale pink t-shirt whose face had been cropped from the pictures. The necklaces were mostly all variations of a chunky silver chain, which held various charms and buttons of all shapes, colors and sizes. I commented one by one on what I liked or didn't like about the pieces, but for the most part I wasn't loving the buttons, so I typed, "Not diggin' the buttons." She sent a couple more pics saying things like, "How about this one?" or, "Is this one any better?"

At that point I started to take a closer look at the pictures, thinking she was wanting me to see something in those necklaces that I just wasn't seeing for some reason. I looked them over again and mentioned that maybe it would help if the woman modeling the necklaces was wearing something other than that "generic pink T-shirt" (my actual words). To which my sweet—and by now exasperated—friend shot back, "That's me, you moron." And the slow-dawning horrible truth hit me: this wasn't a stranger's jewelry I'd been looking at. These were Lori's necklaces, on Lori's neck, and … gulp … Lori's "generic pink T-shirt"! I was speechless. I was appalled at my bluntness and just plain stupidity at not realizing sooner it was Lori in those photos. She said if she'd told me up front she wouldn't have heard my honest opinion, and BOY DID SHE GET IT. I wanted to die.

Boarding that plane in Phoenix, still beet-red with embarrassment, I got on the phone with her and the two of us started convulsing with laughter. Even now we giggle uncontrollably whenever it comes up. But here's the kicker: in spite of me 'not diggin' the buttons', Lori went with her instincts, made several variations of those necklaces, and they ended up being her best-selling pieces. Turns out buttons were a hot commodity. Women loved having them in necklaces *and* bracelets and Lori was savvy enough to find a great little niche with those pieces. It's a good thing she trusted her instincts and not mine. That's the one silver lining in this otherwise humiliating story!

The irony is that often the quirky or unusual aspects of our creative work that we're most unsure and vulnerable about end up being what makes it memorable to others. Not everyone will love it, but it isn't perfection and universal appeal that draws people; it's personality and authenticity. Follow your natural curiosity, focus the lens on something you find interesting or fascinating or beautiful, and then be creative in the ways you invite others to share what you see.

make mistakes

Make interesting mistakes, make amazing mistakes, make glorious and fantastic mistakes.
– Neil Gaiman (author)

MY DAUGHTER, ABBY, HAS BEEN immensely creative since she was just a wee lass. She writes poetry, takes gorgeous photos, writes songs and plays guitar, acts and paints and draws. She's been experimenting with different artistic tracks throughout her teenage years but these days she's settling most passionately — and comfortably — in the songwriting and performing lane. (Insert proud mama smile here) Her approach to creativity is the same as her approach to almost everything in life: she throws herself in, full force, until she's in way over her head, and *then* figures out how to swim. That's my girl.

When Abby was a little girl, before she had any money of her own to buy us birthday or holiday gifts, she would often make things for us out of whatever we had laying around. And when I say 'whatever we had laying around', I'm not talking staci frenes

about a well-stocked assortment of art supplies from Hobby Lobby or Michael's. I'm talking household staples like empty toilet paper rolls, cotton balls, old socks, and macaroni noodles. With a handful of these items, and a fierce look of determination in her eye, she'd get to work in her room on a mystery craft with a flurry of shuffling and scraping and the door firmly shut. Thirty minutes later, she'd emerge with an eclectic little picture frame or treasure box or "whatever-it-was" in hand for one of us, unabashedly thrilled and proud of herself. Not all of it was artsy—or even functional. There were times when my daughter handed me some object that for the life of me I couldn't tell what it was or what its use might be. But she was so eager to please and so confident that we encouraged her to keep making gifts whenever she got the notion. It's what we parents do: slap a magnet on it and stick it on the fridge. Never underestimate the power of Fridge Art!

Here's the thing. Abby still makes gifts for family and friends: cool, funky mixed media cards, abstract paintings for my office, handwritten poems on gorgeous parchment paper, unique frames for her own original photos. The pieces she makes look impressive, professional even, but she still has an eclectic style all her own that I believe she developed early on. She was forced to be über crafty by her not-so-crafty mom's lack of materials. (I craft just like I sew. See Chapter One.) Turns out, necessity *is* the mother of invention. Abby's art developed naturally over the years the more she experimented with new materials and methods, and she was undaunted when they sometimes turned out, well, unusual. In fact, she seemed to embrace the concept that unusual is just someone's random opinion away from avant-garde.

Sister Corita Kent, an artist and teacher in the late '60's, created a now famous list of 'Art Rules' as part of a project for one of her art classes. A favorite of mine is *Rule #6: Nothing is a mistake. There's no win and no fail, only make.* Like so many aspects of creativity, kids often practice this more than adults. Let's face it; most of us are relieved when we get past the messy, work-in-progress stage and have something shiny and polished to show for our efforts. The perfectionist in us out-muscles the risk-taker, and we can sometimes feel compelled to try to fast-track our creative work to the finish line. But we discover in doing so that there's no real shortcut to consistent excellence; we achieve it the old-fashioned way — practice. Time spent working in our area of creativity is invaluable to the sharpening, refining, and yes, even perfecting of our gifts. And with that time needs to come a measure of grace we allow ourselves — to experiment, to risk, and to flounder in uncertainty for a while.

Ira Glass, writer and radio show producer of NPR's *This American Life*, says artists have great taste in the area of their giftedness. It's often why we get into a particular creative area: we have a refined sense of what's "good" and what's not. A chef-in-training knows sumptuous food because she's spent time studying recipes and techniques, and has probably frequented top-rated restaurants and tasted a fair share of gourmet dishes. Most of my musician and songwriter friends share a common admiration for the greats in their field, and aspire to the level of brilliance of, say, a Miles Davis or a John Lennon. In other words, they know good music when they hear it. Writers know good writing. Dancers know good dancing.

Glass points out the huge gap that exists between the work we do in the beginning stages of our creativity and what it's "supposed to look like" in our heads. It's often here that so many of us quit because we can't take the disappointment of seeing our work fall so short of greatness. Many aspiring painters close the door to that spare room and let the canvases and easels collect dust. Guitars sit in corners, strings rusty and out of tune, because after a couple of lessons we can't play like our musical heroes. But Glass points out that it's only in doing volumes and volumes of work that the gap eventually starts closing, and we begin to do work that reaches our own personal standard of excellence.

Once in a while I go digging through the old shoeboxes where I store CDs and even cassette tapes (yep, totally just dated myself) of old songwriting demos. If I'm feeling nostalgic, I'll listen to a few songs I wrote when I was much younger and less experienced. It always elicits a mixed bag of emotions. I cringe at some of the lyrics I wrote that sound so formulaic and cheesy now. And some of the chord changes — probably the only ones I could play at the time! — sound simplistic and predictable now. It's hard to admit to myself that some of the songs I've written are just downright bad, but oh, they are. Still, listening through them is empowering and encouraging. I recommend doing it with your own work if you've saved early sketches, poems, or idea notes over the years. Ultimately, what I hear in those rough recordings is progress. Gradual, for sure; but progress, nonetheless. And the best way I can define that progress is that I eventually got better at writing songs I like to hear.

How did I get there? I don't know, exactly, but Edison's quote about genius being *one percent inspiration and ninety-nine percent perspiration* has always made the most sense to me. Of course, any creative endeavor starts with that elusive and rare treasure: *a good idea*. What sparks it? Anything can. A conversation fragment. A line from a poem. A scene from a movie. A deeply felt emotion that bubbles to the surface unexpectedly. I don't know where the ideas come from, exactly, but I know when they feel promising, and I try to capture those. For years I've carried a small recording device so I can record a melody or lyric or song title when it hits me. It's crucial for me to document the idea when it happens, because sometimes it's fleeting and I forget it. The inspirational idea-chasing is always kind of mysterious and thrilling, like catching a lightning bug in a jar.

Once I've got that bug, the mystery ends and the work begins. After a few weeks or so, I usually have a bunch of little song snippets recorded that I sift through to decide which ones I like enough to develop into full-blown songs. After that comes the sweaty, unglamorous, agonizing, sometimes euphoric, but always strenuous process of working on a song. It's pretty much pure perspiration. It involves playing and singing the idea over and over, adding then subtracting other pieces; tweaking words, melodies, phrases, verses, entire choruses and sometimes tossing out the whole thing altogether and starting over. Then repeating all of that for however long it takes for it to feel "right."

Most songs are works in progress for at least a few days, weeks or months, sometimes longer. Some song ideas I've been trying to finish for five or six years. Songs that I still believe have a great core idea—a catchy melody or a memorable lyric—but for whatever reason, I can't find the right verse or chorus or bridge for it. And the process of working on it, of writing several choruses, coming back to it again and again and trying new ideas, forces me out of my default songwriting mode and into experimental waters. I know that makes me a better songwriter, and only happens with time and a willingness to keep plugging away at different ideas. Even when I want to pull my hair out, or toss the idea out the window and be done with it.

Chuck Close, a professional painter and art instructor, echoes my own experience with the creative process, and reminds me that all of the experimenting and messy tries and start overs eventually lead to a refining of the gift we're responsible for. He writes, *Inspiration is for amateurs — the rest of us just show up and get to work. And believe that things will grow out of the activity itself and that you will — through work — bump into other possibilities and kick open other doors that you would never have dreamt of if you were just sitting around looking for a great 'art idea.'* Let's do the work required to get to the place of excellence that first drew us to this kind of creativity. No cheating, no shortcuts: just keep making.

nothing is wasted

In the morning sow your seed, and at
evening withhold not your hand,
for you do not know which will prosper, this or that, or
whether both alike will be good.
– Ecclesiastes 11:6

WHEN PIXAR CREATED THE HIT animated movie *Brave,* their illustrators worked for months contributing massive quantities of idea sketches for scenes, throwing them on the table with everyone else's ideas to be sorted through and analyzed by the whole crew. As the story began to take shape and took certain twists and turns, the illustrators followed the storyline, working long hours throwing their sketch ideas into the mix. And when it came time to edit, the amount of deleted scenes that didn't make the final cut would have made the movie five times as long, which means that hours and hours of creative, brilliant work were thrown out, and only the cream of the creative crop actually was used. In the end, what we see when we sit in the theater is the best of the best of these thousands of hours of work.

Everything contributing to that final edit counts; none of the work is a waste, because all of it leads, incrementally to the finished product. I've experienced this in songwriting, especially when collaborating with other writers. There's an energy and necessity to getting out as many ideas as possible when we're trying to shape the song into the best possible form. Ideas trigger other ideas, so the more the better. If we're going for a certain rhyming pattern in a song, for example, usually we have to brainstorm for a while before we land on the right words in the right spots. I can never get through this exercise without laughing because inevitably when you're saying any words that come to mind in a certain rhyme scheme you end up with ones that are ridiculous and make no sense with the song. But even the silly words eventually help us get to the right ones.

Accepting the work-in-progress aspect of creativity, even when it's messy and makes us feel vulnerable, develops not only our craft but our character, too. A paradigm shift happens somewhere in the working of our weak areas, much like what happens in the body with muscle growth. Trainers will tell you that our bodies will only develop enough muscle to deal with the load placed on it, and that if we want to see growth we have to work harder with more repetition. And, like our muscles first have to "break down" before they begin to rebuild and strengthen, sometimes our habits and attitudes need breaking in order for us to do better creative work. To quote our friend Sister Corita Kent's *Art Rule #7: The only rule is work. If you work it will lead to something. It's the people who do all of the work all of the time who eventually catch on to things.*

In their book *Art & Fear*, Bayles and Orland tell the story of a ceramics teacher who on the first day of class divided the students into two groups. Group A would be graded on quantity; a scale would weigh the clay pots on grading day, and fifty pounds would earn an "A", forty a "B" and so on. The other half of the class—Group B—would be graded on quality, and only had to turn in one pot, their best effort, on grading day. Group A got right to work, and churned out several pieces throughout the term, learning the craft and fine tuning their skills in the process. Most of Group B, however, spent so much time researching, theorizing and pondering how to create the perfect pot that they had nothing to show for it on grading day. Not surprisingly, the group being graded for quantity produced the highest quality pieces.

You might think the notion of rolling up your sleeves and producing volumes of work for hours and hours contradicts the notion that we need to feel *inspired* to create good work, and you'd be right. Sort of. Keep in mind, I'm not knocking that mysterious one percent inspiration; it's a crucial component without which the song, novel, project, or business wouldn't have sparked our attention in the first place. But as the clay pots experiment illustrates, waiting around to feel inspired often robs us of precious time to get better at our art. Waiting around to feel anything at all about our creative work can sometimes sabotage the whole process and leave us empty-handed. I hate to quote such an overused phrase (thank you, brilliant Nike ad) but, *just do it*.

Steven Pressfield (*The War of Art*) says that those of us who are serious about developing our gifts to their full potential understand that we have to be both trainer and boxer, metaphorically. The boxer's job is to win the fight; everything he is and wants happens in the ring, going rounds against his opponent. The trainer's job is more outside of the ring. The trainer must anticipate the skills needed to win the fight, and to develop those in his boxer. He devises the daily workouts based on the boxer's strengths and most especially, his weaknesses. (Cue the Rocky soundtrack.) We've all seen enough movies to know the trainer has to work his boxer hard, particularly where he's weak, or he's going to get demolished in the ring.

Being both boxer and trainer means that the passion and adrenaline of walking onstage, giving the presentation, hearing the director yell, "Action!" or writing the final draft are only part of the story, only the tip of the iceberg. The countless hours of rehearsing, editing, practicing, preparing that have nothing to do with inspiration and everything to do with hard work, discipline and sweat, are invaluable to those relatively few moments in the limelight. In a very practical sense, being your own trainer means no one's going to tell you to put in the time during those early morning or after-the-kids-have-gone-to-bed hours to work on the skills of your craft. You're it.

A parallel can be drawn here between our creative lives and our spiritual lives. Discipline, focus, and just plain *working out our salvation* (Philippians 2:12) are all a part of the process of developing patience, mercy, joy, peace, goodness, faithfulness — the fruit of the Spirit. From what I've seen in the people closest to me, those characteristics form over time and require practice and repeated behavior to strengthen those "muscles". We don't experience peace naturally in stressful, chaotic circumstances. In fact, it's in those times that *practicing* peace feels like a strenuous workout, and either our peace collapses under the strain, or it gets a little stronger with use. The workout is key; it shows us where we're strong and where we need work. We can't skip it.

Hard work and discipline change us, sharpen us — physically, spiritually, creatively — but it's a slow process. And we're usually the last ones to recognize the changes. We have to trust the process, especially when our gifts and talents are being stretched and expanded — painfully — in a specific work we're called to do by God. The time we spend serving others with our gifts, or working on some of our weak areas in order to be more effective at what we do, is generally thankless and feels endless. In the thick of it, it's often hard to feel any redeeming purpose or transformation happening in us. It's only when we've come out of one of those seasons that we see the growth in ourselves for having gone through it. We see the patience it worked in us, or the forgiveness we had to learn, or the endurance we needed to develop.

I wrote a song for my son when he was in a dark, rough stretch, wrestling with his own demons and trying to get a foothold in the light. He couldn't see it, but I could see he was a work-in-progress. I could see he was transforming, growing, becoming the person he's created to be. There was a divine plan being played out. Ephesians 2 reminded me that Zach is God's work of art, created for a purpose — and that involves shaping and refining him to become his best self. I'm grateful God approaches us with the persistence and care of an artist *who started this great work in you and will keep at it and bring it to a flourishing finish on the very day Christ Jesus appears.* (Philippians 1:6)

More Like Your Father Every Day

It's a struggle
It's so hard
Trying to make your way
All your troubles
Tears and scars
Seem to be in vain
But I can see a faint familiar light
Rising in your face
Through the hard fights
Desperate dark nights
When you knew your heart would break
Love was making
Something breath-taking
Now you're standing here today
Looking more like your father every day
More like your father every day
Don't you worry
That's just life
Shaping who you are
Sure and steady
It takes time
To make a perfect heart
I can see a better kind of you
Rising from your pain

…

I see him in you
Making all things new

You're looking more
More like your father
Looking more
More like your father
Looking more
Like your father
Every day

seek connection

Nothing ventured, nothing gained
and I only have myself to blame
– from "No Tomorrow" *(Staci Frenes, Kenon Chen)*

IF IT'S NOT OBVIOUS BY now, I'll just come out and confess that I'm pretty much your textbook introvert. I refuel when I'm by myself, and alone tends to be my default comfort zone. When I'm not traveling, I work from home and don't interact much with people in the normal course of my day. I have a few close friends with whom I email or text during the week, but most days I'm flying solo after my hubby goes to work and the kids are out doing their thing. I'm generally quiet, not very good at small talk, and I often feel I'm better with people at arm's length than close relationships. In fact, I probably took to performing because of the natural barrier it creates. It allows me to share about myself in a way that I control and doesn't involve much risk. (Whew, I feel better now. Can we still be friends?)

I've already told you I'm a sucker for poetry,

and if you skip reading the poem below (and you know who you are) I forgive you. But it's a good one. I discovered it in college and have come back to it a few times over the years because it reminds me of my need for connection with others. Something I don't naturally nurture.

A Noiseless Patient Spider

Walt Whitman

A noiseless patient spider,
I marked where on a little promontory it stood isolated,
Marked how to explore the vacant, vast surrounding,
It launched forth filament, filament, filament, out of itself.
Ever unreeling them, ever tirelessly speeding them.
And you O my soul where you stand,
Surrounded, detached, in measureless oceans of space,
Ceaselessly musing, venturing, throwing, seeking the
spheres to connect them.
Till the bridge you will need be formed,
till the ductile anchor hold,
Till the gossamer thread you fling catch somewhere,
O my soul.

The spider in this poem launches his little spi-dey-threads, attaching himself to the world around him, and introverts like me have to wonder why he does this, when it's so much easier and safer not to.

The threads we fling as human beings are delicate emotions we risk sharing and hope will find solid catch, not leave us hanging in mid-air. The things that connect us are the very things that make us feel most vulnerable: illogical fears, repeat struggles, secret dreams—things we'd rather keep close, maybe even hidden. To seek connection is to constantly risk being misunderstood, ignored ... rejected. For me it requires a conscious effort at every turn.

I'm getting better, though. When I do reach out and spend time with people I care about, I experience their gifts in unexpected and profound ways, more than I can count. Sometimes a coffee or lunch date with girlfriends—particularly when I'm hurting or feeling isolated—is a powerful reminder of how much I need the perspectives of others. My friend Christy brings laughter to even the most serious moments, and Stephanie's compassionate and tender heart is always ready with a kind word of encouragement. Mandi helps me to take a few steps back and see the bigger picture—whatever the context, and Lori is the kindest soul and best listener I know. I need what each one of these lovely women, and others, brings to my life.

I have a couple of therapist friends I've called on when I've been worried and stressed beyond what I could manage, and they've navigated me to a place where I could breathe easier and feel more hopeful. I remember one particular late-night conversation in my friend Candace's kitchen where I poured out my jumbled, confused thoughts about a painful situation I was going through. I was a mess; nothing coming out of my mouth was making any sense and I knew it. Over several hours Candace calmly asked questions without offering opinion or judgment, and answering made me collect and sort through my thoughts—something I hadn't been able to do before then. Sometime around two o'clock that morning, I remember thinking: *I can get through this. I'm not going to have a mental breakdown.* I don't think I could have arrived at that place on my own. I needed her particular insightfulness and wisdom—distinct gifts that make her so good at her job.

If I remain detached I miss out on the benefits—encouragement, companionship, laughter, advice—things only those with whom I'm connected can give me. If I don't build those bridges between others and myself I have nowhere to travel, and no one can get to me. We can apply the same principle in our areas of creativity. Artists in a variety of fields would likely agree that they tend to be more comfortable working alone, and that tendency can often lead to loneliness and isolation. Working collaboratively isn't always an easy practice. It's less distracting, less intimidating to create alone. We don't have to answer to anyone else, or connect what we're doing with anyone else's work. Working with others means we have to trust others, and that involves letting go of the need to control. But there are payoffs to relinquishing all of the control: we open ourselves to valuable input and feedback needed for our work to grow.

When I got my first music publishing deal, which involved writing songs for a publisher to pitch to other artists, it was suggested that I collaborate with other songwriters. The idea was that in the meeting of two or three creative minds, there'd be potential for writing songs I might not otherwise write on my own. I was game—but I was also scared to death. I'd have to bring my personal song ideas and lyrics into a writing session, and it was going to feel like reading my junior high diary out loud in front of a stranger. Seriously awkward, frightening, and potentially all-out humiliating if no one liked my ideas.

My first collaborative writing session was as intimidating and uncomfortable as I'd feared. I'd been told beforehand to come prepared to toss all of my melody and lyric ideas into the ring, not just the ones I thought were great; to engage in musical brainstorming, basically. The other writer was good at it. He quickly threw out lines and melodies that all sounded like good options for the song we were working on. He kept the entire session moving forward while I sat in a ball of paralysis telling myself every single idea that popped into my head was too dumb, obvious, simple, etc. to say out loud. He must have thought I was completely useless—and I truly was. I was so afraid of what he'd think that I kept all of my ideas to myself.

Later, as I got more comfortable with my own writing, being in a room and thinking out loud with other writers became easier. Without a steady flow of unedited and sometimes silly and impossible ideas, we may never get to the really good ones. I learned— and am still learning—from those collaborative efforts an invaluable lesson: *I need other people.* I am not a lone ranger, and in fact, I often do my best work in the interplay that happens in a collaborative effort. My strengths in the songwriting process are lyrics and melody. (Surprised?) So the best collaborators for me often bring something to the process that I'm lacking—usually a strong instrumental music writer is my best fit.

Working with people who have different strengths has at least two benefits, in my experience: it almost always improves the quality of the project and it forces us to think outside the boundaries of our own comfort zone. I have learned volumes of valuable wisdom from the talented songwriters I've worked with; wisdom I apply to every new song I write. They enlarge me, creatively. I've also seen how the project—the song, in my case—is often better served when I'm open to collaborating. There's a value in getting one's ego and sense of exclusive ownership out of the way. It becomes less about the individual creator and more about the end product.

I've been dabbling in the world of book editing for a year or so. At first I just did a few final read-throughs of manuscripts for an editor friend of mine, then started doing some on my own. I've learned about a valuable practice among writers that I think would be helpful in any creative field. Many authors rely on "beta readers" to read early drafts of the book and provide feedback while it's still in progress. Beta readers are usually trusted friends who are either writers themselves or just lovers of the genre. Sometimes authors send the entire manuscript to the beta readers before it goes to an editor or publisher, and sometimes they'll send a few chapters at a time while writing it. Either way, it's a crucial stage in the process. The best beta readers read thoughtfully and have a no-holds-barred honesty policy that's invaluable to the writer.

I've read manuscripts that have skipped the beta reader stage, and every one of them could have *greatly* benefited from it. Writers, like creators in any field, can easily get lost inside their own bubbles where the tendency is either to become hyper-critical and insecure (which can lead to creative paralysis), or lazy and impatient (which can lead to shortcuts and subpar work). It requires a letting go, a vulnerability, to share a work in progress, to invite feedback and insight early on. If we're not letting in the insight of collaborators, mentors or even objective friends while our work is still taking shape, it can suffer from our own myopia and short-sightedness. The risk we take when connecting with others in the creative process is far outweighed by what we gain in perspective.

Iron sharpens iron; and one man sharpens another (Proverbs 27:17) is a truth we need to recognize and aspire to in our creative lives. Collaborating with others enlarges our perspective and sharpens our appreciation for each part that makes up the whole. And it requires recognition of our basic human need for connection. Like that spider in the poem, I don't want to do life without the bonds of loving relationships leading to and from my heart, and I don't want to do my creative work without the valuable insights of trusted colleagues and friends. I need to remember to keep flinging my spider webs across the distance that isolates me from others.

play your part

As each one does its part,
the body grows in love
– Ephesians 4:16

ONE OF THE COOLEST EXPERIENCES I know is playing in a band. The taste for it dates way back to when I was a kid holding a hairbrush like a microphone in front of the bathroom mirror. I imagined myself a rocker chick like Nancy Wilson of Heart, or Pat Benatar; the lights pulsing, the crowd cheering, the smoke rising from the stage and the band poised to hit the down beat just as I step into the spotlight and belt out the opening song. Surely you've had a similar fantasy. Anybody else ... besides me? Hello? Testing ... one ... two ... three...

I haven't experienced that *exact rock-star* scenario, but I know a little about being in bands. Since high school I've been playing in bands of one kind or another, and the experience is hard to put into words. It's a feeling of shared respect, trust, energy, and some kind of inexplicable *mojo* when everyone is

playing together in the same groove. It's unlike anything I've ever known. It's transcendent when it's
working, but can also be a train wreck when it's not.
The difference is sometimes a fine line, sometimes a
wide gap, but is usually determined by the confidence and ability of each player to contribute to the
whole—essentially *owning* their specific part and giving everyone else the space and confidence needed to
play *their* part.

Confession: I'm not the best guitar player in the
world. In fact, I often jokingly dub myself "The
Camp Counselor" because holding down a basic
"Kumbaya" rhythm is about as fancy as my playing
gets. My musicianship is passable, but not what I'd
consider my strength, or the foot I lead with in a
band situation. My strength is a combination of factors. In my own band, as the primary songwriter I
know the material better than anyone else (hopefully!). As the lead singer, I set the tone for the style and
feel of the music. As the rhythm acoustic guitar player, I bring the basic meat-n-potatoes parts, leaving
the gravy to the lead guitarist. I know what I do fairly well, and I've learned what I *don't* do well. My role
in the band has been forged by trial and error in the
several years I've spent learning my strengths and
limitations with a group of other musicians.

I've seen the band U2's live show a couple of
times and it's a spiritual experience I compare to
church—powerful, soul-moving, spirit-lifting. Bono

plays his lead role with the passion and flair of a true rock star, and he's given free rein and support by the solid and brilliant performances of his three band mates. The spotlight shines on each of them at different times throughout the show, allowing them to shred or rip or whatever it is they do, while the others step back in the arrangement during those moments, giving their full attention and respect. Each one owns his part, and the whole is magnificent. They're a well-oiled machine of a rock band, and the result is unprecedented success and consistently sold-out shows.

I've also seen organizations, teams and even partners be "rock stars" in their own field, working together in a way that makes room for one another's gifts, accomplishing more together than any one could alone. Cultivating a creative life involves understanding our essential role "in the band" or in community, and recognizing how our own mosaic piece fits alongside others to complete the work we're each called to do. It means believing that what we each bring—our offering of talent, resources, opportunities, skills—is crucial to the functioning of the group, our colleagues, our creative or faith community.

My friend TJ was the drummer of a band I played with in college. He now has four kids, all of whom have various levels of interest and talent in music. He and his wife homeschool their kids and TJ does a lesson in music collaboration that I think is brilliant. To start, he puts each of his kids on their instrument of choice — piano, drums, guitar, bass — and gives them a song to play together. Then he switches them all to a new instrument to play the same song. He rotates them again until they've played the song on all four instruments. What happens, TJ tells me, is that the kids are forced to pay closer attention to what the others are playing in order to stay in sync. As a result, they listen to music more informed (and appreciative) about how each part contributes to the sound.

Collaborating in any creative endeavor works best when we each do like the old song says — *put our whole selves in* — along with a healthy dose of respect and gratitude for everyone else who has also put in. Scripture reminds us we are not alone but part of a community of believers, and as such we contribute by bringing all of who we are, the gifts and talents we possess, when we come together.

When you gather for worship, each one of you be prepared with something that will be useful for all: Sing a hymn, teach a lesson, tell a story, lead a prayer, provide an insight. (1 Corinthians 14:26)

Notice the array of talents — music, teaching, storytelling, praying, counseling — offered for the good of all when believers gather for worship. No one is given more honor or attention than another, even though we often fall into the trap of creating classes of distinction according to what gifts we deem more or less important. There's no mistaking the phrase "each of you" here: whatever our gift or talent, to the extent that we don't come prepared to share it, we lessen the richness of the worship experience for others.

As Christ followers, our community includes not only our circle of friends or work colleagues or writer's group—it's the whole Church, the Body of Christ of which we are all members. In 1 Corinthians 12 Paul makes a beautiful case for the interdependence of each member being key to the health of the whole. We bring our piece of stained glass to the window and it fits into place, filling in the narrative of God's story being told through us and those around us. In seclusion and isolation it's sometimes hard to see the greater significance of what we do, like seeing a single jigsaw puzzle piece apart from the whole. Some of the distinct gifts God gives us find their bigger purpose more in community than in isolation.

Scripture tells the story of a particular creative community working together on a project bigger and broader in scope than they could ever have achieved individually. It's a beautiful picture of checking egos at the door, Old Testament-style. It involves a diverse array of skilled artists bringing their talents to build the tabernacle, a place for the presence of God to dwell among His people in the wilderness. Notice the collaborative spirit in Peterson's translation (*The Message*) of Exodus 35: 20-24:

Everyone whose heart stirred him to action and everyone whose spirit was willing came and brought the offering for the Lord for the work of the tent of meeting, for all its service, and for the holy garments. They came, men and women alike, all who had willing hearts … Everyone making an offering of silver or bronze brought it as an offering to the Lord, and everyone who had acacia wood for any work of the service brought it. Every woman who was skilled spun with her hands and brought what she had spun, blue, purple, or scarlet yarn, or fine linen, and all the women whose heart stirred them to action and who were skilled spun goats' hair … The Israelites brought a freewill offering to the Lord, every man and woman whose heart was willing to bring materials for all the work that the Lord through Moses had commanded them to do.

Look at all the mentions of "willing" hearts in this passage! I love the richness in the specificity of various kinds of workmanship, too: the woodworker, the goldsmith and my personal favorite, the goats' hair spinner. All would be considered highly skilled artists in their field, and yet the overall impression is not just one of industrious productivity but joyous collaboration. The artists are s*tirred to action* to work alongside one another. No one is coaxing or guilting anyone to contribute. Healthy communities inspire us to bring our best, not because we feel obligated to do so, but because we are naturally stirred to offer our talents alongside others who are equally invested in something greater than any one of us could achieve on our own. All of the talents, gifts, offerings and skills involved in this process culminate not in a stone statue or empty museum, but in a meeting place between God and His people, an intersection of heaven and earth, alive with His presence, full of His glory to be seen in the midst of those who gather to meet Him there.

Jesus tells us in Matthew's gospel, *Where two or more are gathered in my name there I am in the midst of them.* God dwells in our gatherings when our hearts are knit together in love and oneness of purpose, setting aside any agenda other than seeking and honoring Him. And to those gatherings we bring our full selves, gifts and talents, offering them for the good of all. Paul picks up on this theme in Ephesians, reminding us, *God is building a home ... using you, fitting you in brick by brick, stone by stone, with Christ Jesus as the cornerstone that holds all the parts together ... a temple in which God is quite at home. (2:20-22)*

The 'stones' we contribute are the distinct gifts we offer one another in all of life's experience, not just in the places and times we call "church". We do what we each do in community, without holding back, without burying or hiding what we have. And God wants to be a part of it. He wants to make His home right there in the midst of our imperfect, broken lives so he can fill us and equip us to work alongside Him. When we contribute willingly, freely, stirred to action by the greatness and bigness of His vision and His heart, we feel what it's like to play the instrument only we can play in the band—the great big beautiful band that is the Body of Christ.

creative practices: cultivate your fields

Reader Reflection Questions

Have you discovered a 'flow' in your area of creativity? Or are you in a season where you're not experiencing energy or passion in what you do, and you're looking to reconnect with it? If so, think about why, and how you can make some time to do what you love.

Do you know what keeps your heart from breaking? When you experience pain or disappointment or loss do you find comfort in an activity related to your creativity?

What sort of websites, books, videos or even conversations pique your interest? List them, if you're journaling. Think about those areas of interest where your natural curiosity takes you, and how they may relate to your strengths and areas of creativity.

How would your best friend or closest family member describe your personality 'quirks'? What do you think makes your personality different, unique? Do you see those things as assets or flaws? How do your distinct per-

sonality traits show up in your creativity?

Who are the people in your creative field that inspire you? What is it about the work they do that's inspiring? Do you see yourself as a work-in-progress toward the level of excellence that you aspire to?

How many hours in an average week do you spend actually doing something creative in your area of gifting? Think about where you could create some time and space to do more 'volume' in order to bridge the gap between where you want to be and where you are now.

List 3 people you know and trust who share your area of creativity. Have you made connections with them in some way? Collaborated? Mentored? Consider ways you can give and receive more encouragement and helpful critiques from them in order to sharpen one another's skills and talents.

creative action:
sow and reap

commit

We are each given unique wings with unique
particulars of how to use our wings;
no one else can fly for you. You have to jump off the edge,
and spread your wings.
—Makoto Fujimura (painter)

MY FRIEND, JEN, 23, IS a kindred creative soul who recently graduated with a degree in film studies and now works for DreamWorks Studios in San Francisco, a long way from her native Georgia home. When we first met, I asked how she ended up all the way out here on the West Coast. She told me that after graduating she'd applied for 32 different internships and DreamWorks was the only one that responded— and with an unpaid position to boot. Without knowing a soul in San Francisco, and with very little money in her bank account, Jen accepted the internship, then hoped and prayed like crazy that she'd be able to make it work. The cost of living in San Francisco is a lot higher than rural Georgia, but she was determined to make the move, even if she had to live in the worst part of town to keep the internship. She saved what little money she had and kept praying for provision.

It came in the form of a phone call not too long before she was supposed to leave for California. Turns out, Jen had entered her name in a drawing months earlier at her local Regal Cinemas and she'd won the grand prize—$4,000! It paid for her move and lodging for a few months. When the Dream-Works internship was over, Jen felt sure they'd offer her a position, which they did. It was in the mail-room, where, bless her heart, she worked faithfully for a few months, all the while praying for a chance to prove herself in a more creative position. It, too, came. Her supervisor approached her with an offer to serve in a central communications role between several departments working on the upcoming film, *Penguins.* It's more than she'd hoped for. The job al-lows her the golden opportunity to see how all the different creative facets work together on a movie— the best kind of training there is for what she wants to do.

I couldn't stop smiling while Jen first told me her story. I love God's miraculous provision! I also love Jen's gutsy decision to move across the continent, following her heart in the face of so many unknowns. Even with that prize money, Jen had to find an apartment and make a life for herself in a huge city where she knew no one. In less than a year, she'd managed to connect with a healthy church and make a few good friends. The kicker is she's also writing a book about this past year of her life, wanting to offer her own insights and story to other young women transitioning from college to the "real world". I adore her.

Whatever our area of talent, and whatever the stage of readiness we feel in putting it to use, there's a pivotal point at which we have to make the decision to fly, because as the quote above suggests, no one else can do it for us. Our gifts require action, investment, and application. Until then, it's all just practice, brainstorming and dress rehearsal. Jen's story reminds me of this quote from the explorer W.H. Murray about commitment:

Until one is committed, there is hesitancy, the chance to draw back ... the moment one definitely commits oneself, then providence moves too. A whole stream of events issues from the decision, raising in one's favor all manner of unforeseen incidents, meetings and material assistance, which no man could have dreamt would have come his way. – **The Scottish Himalayan Expedition**

The million-dollar line for me is this: ...*the moment one definitely commits oneself, then providence moves too.* Commitment says, "I'm willing to overcome any obstacle in my path—no matter how long it takes or how difficult the process." It's stepping into the boat, however rough the waters, mysterious the destination or unstable the vessel. It's the leap of faith that takes us from *trying* to *doing*. And with that leap, Murray claims, heaven itself gets on board, orchestrating *all manner of unforeseen incidents, meetings and material assistance.*

There's something about that concept of provision following commitment that both defies logic and makes perfect sense. What seems impossible, daunting, risky, frightening, etc. suddenly seems less so once you take that first step to commit, like Jen accepting an internship across the country. All the hours spent practicing, rehearsing, praying and planning have equipped you for this unique thing you're about to do, and as you begin to actually DO it, the miracle of strength, wisdom, and more resources than you could have imagined undergirds you.

There's a story in Scripture I've drawn inspiration from over and over in my creative and spiritual life. It reminds me that this act of committing is essential, even in the face of impossible odds. Jesus has been healing the sick and teaching on a hillside to a large crowd of over five thousand men—at least twice that counting women and children—that have followed and listened to him for several hours. When night starts to fall the disciples tell Jesus to send the people away, but Jesus knows they're hungry and wants to feed them. He tells his disciples to find food, but one look around the remote location reveals no source of food large enough to feed so many. You get the sense that Jesus knows this, and the disciples know he knows, but they report back to him anyway, telling him there is no food.

Jesus gets wind that there's a young boy with a basket containing a few loaves of bread and two fish—an unlikely solution to this dilemma, and probably one the disciples overlooked. Jesus tells his disciples to bring him this basket; he breaks the bread and gives thanks, and then tells his disciples to distribute it to the hungry crowd. There's no record that the disciples turn to Jesus at this point and ask Him if he is out of His mind. I might have been the Doubting Thomas in that scenario, asking sheepishly, "Um, excuse me, Jesus, but I don't think you did the math right?" I'd have turned to face that huge crowd with a few hunks of bread in my hands, shaking in my sandals, too scared to move and too scared not to move. But the disciples do what Jesus asks, feeding the five thousand with those meager resources, and not only is there enough to go around, there are leftovers—twelve baskets full.

Sometimes we feel like we're holding a basket of just a few loaves and fish at the start of a big creative endeavor. We believe we're in the right place, doing the right thing, hearing from God, but nevertheless feeling the absolutely overwhelming sense that there just *won't be enough* to get the thing done—not enough money, not enough energy, not enough talent, not enough time, not enough help from God who first called us to the work! It's a scary thing to begin walking into the crowd handing out what little we have, digging into the bottom of that basket for more, more, more when we can see with our eyes there just isn't enough. We need to acknowledge and allow ourselves to feel that panic, because if we're ever going to do work that matters we need to get used to it and keep creating anyway.

I've learned that when you're starting a big project you know God has called you to it's sometimes better to not do the math. As an independent musician without the partnership of a record label, I've released several albums over the course of my career. Each of them has cost a hefty sum to record, mix, master, manufacture and market. That hefty sum has to be paid by us — my husband and me — who essentially are the record label. Over the years I'm not sure how we've managed to scrape the budgets together for these albums with what we had in savings, or what we could pay month to month on a loan, or from generous people who believed in our ministry. But I can honestly say that each and every time we decide to make another record, we feel just like one of those disciples looking into our basket of meager provisions.

The hard part is to start the project anyway, in spite of those meager provisions, distributing what we have in faith that the work itself is bigger than our own intellect. I begin writing the songs, talking to my producer, blocking out time on my calendar. Sometimes before I even have the whole budget part figured out. This is a tricky thing. Because your mind — and well-meaning friends — will often tell you you're being foolish, you're being irresponsible; you're taking a risk which may never pay off. But you know in the deepest part of your heart this is what you're called to do and unless you take the first scary steps out into the crowd with what you've got, you're never going to see the boundless provision of God in it. That first step is one of the most difficult, but essential, works of art you will ever do.

Jesus could've provided food for that crowd of 5,000+ with a lot more drama and fanfare than he chose to that day. This is the Son of the same God who'd sent down manna from heaven to feed His people in the desert. The same God who'd told Moses to strike a rock with His rod and water flowed out. Instead, He asked His followers to be His hands and feet, joining Him in providing for the hungry thousands, impossible as it looked. It's as though He wanted them to experience that kind of faith that can only develop in the face of a seeming impossibility. I believe the extraordinary happens when we commit, when we actually take those momentous or baby steps with our gifts. Somehow the act of leaning into the work we're called to do with the full force of our hearts and our faith and our will generates the miracle of provision and resources—whatever they may be.

> *With a leap of faith I jump across*
> *to the other side*
> *So much to gain compared to all I leave behind*
> *I'm not afraid I know there's love*
> *on the other side*
> *So I'll cross this great divide*
> *I'll cross the great divide*

(From "The Great Divide" Staci Frenes © 2004 Stone's Throw Music/ASCAP)

momentum

When you're in a rut
you have to question everything
except your ability to get out of it.
– Twyla Tharp (dancer, choreographer)

I WAS AT LUNCH WITH a few friends and as we munched on appetizers and sipped our drinks, we talked about a common struggle many of us have in regards to the creative life; finishing the things we start. I'd read in Donald Miller's book *A Million Miles in a Thousand Years* a line that stayed with me: *Thinking about creating is not the same as creating.* I said to my friends, "You know, when it comes right down to it there is no trying. There's only doing something or not doing it, right?" Everyone nodded but we all felt a bit squirmy and convicted about it because, let's face it, 'try' is a common semantic loophole we like to use when we don't want to fully commit. We'll say, "I'm going to *try* and finish that website this weekend!" Or, "I'm *trying* to start exercising again!" because it leaves us some wiggle room in case we don't actually do it.

Perhaps the most important step in cultivating a creative life is where the proverbial rubber hits the road. It's the moment we take our ideas and put them into action. Twyla Tharp, in her wonderful book *The Creative Habit* calls it taking our verbs and turning them into nouns. For example, taking our writing(v) to a book(n), or our developing(v) to a website(n). Nouns are concrete, solid, final. And there's a comforting appeal to *not* wrestle down an especially big, messy and daunting project into a finished product. We'd rather allow ourselves the luxury of a million conversations with friends about what we *might do*, what we're thinking of *trying*, what would be interesting to *explore,* because it feels impossible at times to take it from starting point to the finish line.

There are a lot of reasons we stall out at the beginning or even middle of a project. The most obvious is that it's easier to talk about it than to do the work it takes to finish it. But more deep-seated issues like fear and resistance — those things that first keep us from uncovering our gifts — also hinder us from taking decisive action with it. The critical self-talk in our head reaches a deafening crescendo the closer we get to the finish line. *What if no one likes it? Or no one cares? What if all the expectations I have for it won't be realized?* Too often the questions win out, paralyze us, and the idea gets stuck in the Planning and Talking About It stage. Which is comfortable and safe, but in the end results in us being stuck and the work staying buried.

At about this point in our lunch conversation my friend Barbara threw her napkin on the table and confessed, "That's it. I guess I'm going to have to finish it now." There was a long pregnant pause as we looked at her, waiting for the rest of the story. Turns out, unbeknownst to us, Barbara, a writing and research specialist at a law firm, was writing a novel — a suspense thriller! Looking around sheepishly at our shocked faces, she explained that the book was an idea she and a friend had been discussing for a couple of years, and they'd finally taken the plunge and begun writing several months earlier. They'd written 18 chapters, then for various reasons they'd come to a screeching halt. To which I think I spoke for the whole group when I said, incredulously, "And we haven't heard about this book *because*…"

Barbara breathed a big sigh, and out it came — the full disclosure, the true confession, the list of excuses which, even as she was telling them, started losing steam and she knew it. The biggest reason she hadn't told us about the book, of course, was that she'd wanted to finish it first. Sharing a work-in-progress is a frightening proposition for veteran writers, never mind a first time novelist. She'd been keeping a tight lid on it until then. The problem, though, was that since no one knew about it, it was easy for her to let it sit on her hard drive, untouched. Indefinitely. Apparently, the other writer bailed on the project early on, and that derailed a lot of Barbara's initial enthusiasm. What followed was one unfortunate distraction after another, including a season of longer than usual work hours, some health problems, and just plain discouragement. She admitted that she was stuck, and had been for some time. She also admitted that she knew she needed to finish it. It had been a longtime dream of hers to write a novel, and she didn't want to see it die just because she'd gotten stuck in a rut.

As the former English teacher in the bunch, I told her in my no-nonsense teacher voice to promptly send me the first 18 chapters so I could read them, which she did. My thinking was that just knowing someone was reading what she had written so far would get Barbara's juices stirring again. I stayed up until two a.m. reading those chapters that night—genuinely hooked and eager to find out what happened next in her story. I told her so, and soon after that she got into a rhythm of writing again. I found new chapters in my inbox weekly for the next couple of months and was thrilled when I read that final page with the words "The End" written across it. She'd done it.

Not only did Barbara finish writing the book, she published it and *Dark Work* is now available on Amazon.com. I'm sure she'd love to sell a million

copies, get rich and travel the world as a famous author. But, honestly? I think the joy of *completing* her
first novel was a huge reward in itself. We were all
incredibly proud of her, and as we talked in the
weeks following the publication, Barbara told me
how liberating and empowering it was to finally get
over the hump of her own discouragement and begin
writing again. The longer she'd left it alone, the easier it was to forget about its existence and push it to
the bottom of the day's list of things to do.

Like a stiff muscle from not enough use, our creativity also suffers badly from inertia. Newton's First
Law of Motion confirms it: the tendency of a body in
motion is to keep moving; the tendency of a body at
rest is to sit still. It's a lot less work to *keep* moving
once you have some momentum than it is to *start*
moving from a dead stop. When facing what feels
like an insurmountable creative project, start with the
easiest step you can imagine. In Barbara's case it was
sending me an email of the chapters she had already
written. From there, it was a series of small steps that
took her to the place where she was ready to begin
digging in again. When you're stuck in a rut, any
movement is good movement at first. Once you start
moving, you'll feel unbelievably better. Your foot
touches the ground and you feel the power of motion, and possibly even that rut moving behind you.
That one step — it's a doozy.

I heard a fascinating interview on NPR radio

with a neurologist named Oliver Sacks who had been conducting studies about the relationship between music and the human brain for his book, *Musicophil-ia*. One of his more famous case studies involved Clive Wearing, a brilliant pianist, conductor, and musicologist whose memory was erased almost entirely after a severe and rare brain infection. After the trauma of the infection, Clive's short-term memory lasted just a few seconds and he couldn't form any long-term memories. He could remember almost nothing unless he was actually doing it, and even then it would only sometimes come to him.

But Sacks explained that Clive's "musical self", the part that actually performed music, remained almost completely intact. It just needed activating. When he was playing music or conducting a choir, Clive could access the specific skills and expertise needed to perform even the most difficult pieces he'd played before his brain injury. When he played piano or conducted, he had no actual memory of his extensive musical background or education. It's just that his fingers and his mind, once in motion, knew what to do. The momentum of the music carried him from note to note, bar to bar.

The story illustrates in an extreme context how the power of momentum—starting with even a small, easy step when we're stuck—moves us forward. When we focus on just the task right in front of us, without pausing at every distraction, from wondering what's in the refrigerator to other people's criticism of our work, it's much easier to stay in motion. Discouragement and our own inner critic can especially slow us down. Doubting our ability to succeed, questioning our motives, pointing out the unlikelihood of ever finishing the project—there are a million different ways we sabotage our own momentum. But like Clive with his fingers on the piano keys or Barbara plugging away, chapter by chapter, it's crucial to our "creativity muscles" that we keep moving, accomplishing the next small step in the process without continually trying to envision the whole.

Getting stuck creatively is a lot like getting stuck emotionally or physically. Obsessing about the big picture is counter-productive and doesn't help one bit. We end up staring at our lofty goals while firmly entrenched in a rut. Deciding to lose 30 pounds is a lot more daunting than deciding to go for a walk. It's the same with a creative project. Building a multi-page website, writing a semester curriculum unit, producing a play—these are big, messy, overwhelming creative endeavors. Even a small bit of motion creates momentum. If we can break down the End Result into actions steps that can be taken daily, or even weekly, we find a rhythm that gets us up and out of our rut and into a groove. Once we're in a groove, it's hard to stop. We're fluid, warmed up, using the muscles of our creativity and seeing results.

follow your (broken) heart

The best thing a man can do
is love until his heart breaks.
– Wendell Barry (author)

I WAS IN THE SANTA Cruz Mountains one weekend speaking at a women's conference about the Parable of the Talents. We were focusing especially on
the themes of loving others in practical ways through
our gifts, and I was thrilled to both encourage and
hear about the different ways these women were already serving in their areas of giftedness. But something in particular happened during one of the sessions that will remain imprinted in my memory as a
beautiful illustration of the ways we can love each
other with our unique talents.

A young Syrian woman ("Lilith") had been invited to the conference at the last minute, and everyone seemed surprised and delighted that she'd actually come. Just a few days earlier, Lilith had fled her
country and found refuge with one of the women
attending the conference. As an Orthodox Christian

in Syria, she and her loved ones had become targets of violent atrocities from radical terrorist groups in the country's ongoing civil war. Lilith had witnessed horrors no one her young age should ever see. Despite the further danger it presented, she'd decided to leave her home and her family to find safety here in America. Knowing some of her story, and seeing her sitting through the sessions at the retreat, head covered in a scarf, face bowed toward the floor, broke my heart.

Lilith's story touched all of us, including Pam, an attendee who was a quilt maker. The beautiful, hand stitched old-fashioned kind you don't find too many people making anymore. Pam and I talked that first night of the conference and I learned that she made quilts for Project Linus, an organization that donates handcrafted quilts and blankets to children who are seriously ill, traumatized, or otherwise in need. Pam told me she'd been making quilts for her friends and family for years, but it was when she'd studied the Parable of the Talents on her own that she was moved to do more. She told me, "I saw how the two servants in the story used what they had and thought, 'You either do it or you don't. So I did it!'" I hugged her hard. She gets it.

Pam had just finished a gorgeous, intricately-patterned quilt she'd been inspired to create at one of the past women's retreats, and had brought it with her. She, along with a few of the leaders, decided to give it to Lilith as a symbol of their comfort and love. Lilith had left her own mother behind in her homeland, and I can't imagine how frightened and alone she felt, but in her absence I could see there were lots of "mamas" in this community of women who were more than ready to love on her. During our last session together Lilith was called forward and prayed over, hugged, and wrapped up in that beautiful quilt. I thought of the many hours Pam undoubtedly spent working on it, unaware of the horrendous events that would lead Lilith to this moment—literally surrounded by the beauty and love the quilt embodied. I wept. When they told her it was for her, she wept. We all wept, honking our noses and wiping our eyes.

I thought about the words from 1 Peter 4:10: *Serve one another with the particular gifts God has given each of you, as faithful dispensers of the magnificently varied grace of God.* The words *particular* and *varied* suggest to me that there may be as many gifts as there are people and personalities. A quilt wrapped around a ravaged young woman that says, "God is with you, and we're here for you" is just one practical, loving act of service that demonstrates God's grace. Think of all of the multi-talented and variously gifted people you know. The ways they manifest strength, personality, and flavor in what they do. Now think of just as many hurting, suffering people you're aware of—right now, today. Imagine the ways these gifts could intersect with these needs, and see the wisdom in Paul's words in this verse. *Serve one another with the particular gifts God has given you.*

Paraphrasing one of my favorite writers, Frederick Buechner, I believe we find our true calling at that intersection where our greatest passion meets the world's need. When we feel moved to compassion by something in particular that's in tune with our personality and sensibility, we ought to pay attention. What breaks our heart is as much an indicator of our calling as what brings us our deepest joy. We will find ourselves moved by some kinds of suffering more than others. Often the overwhelming emotion we experience in the face of that suffering is the Spirit of God longing to comfort, heal, or encourage, saying, "Those are your fields—sow yourself like seed *there.*" And we know we're gifted and equipped to offer help in ways that are especially unique to us.

Around the time I started writing this book my dad passed away unexpectedly from cancer. It took him fast and hard, plunging those of us who loved him into that particular pain you experience when you're not prepared for death. Like all of us, Dad's best friend of over 40 years, Ray, was devastated. He felt helpless with grief and despair, yet wanted to convey in some tangible way how sorry he was for our loss and how deeply he loved and missed my dad. He's an artist and a man of few words, so he set quietly to work on a project in his studio.

Ray and my dad had shared a love of travel and photography. At the beach they often found washed up pieces of driftwood that made for great photos. Some of the smaller and more interesting pieces they'd sometimes bring home. One of these pieces of driftwood they'd brought home looked like a minia-ture tree with several intricate branches that split and forked near the top into even smaller branches—as thin as twigs. He started working on that piece, treat-ing it with protective varnish to keep it from cracking or splitting, then mounted it onto a thick slab of black marble for balance and stability. He then painstak-ingly attached a small clear crystal bead to the tip of each delicate branch until the whole tree was covered with them.

I wish you could see this tree sculpture—it's a gorgeous work of art. It stands about two and a half feet high on my mom's mantelpiece; the little crystal tips catch light from all over the room and reflect it back in exquisite patterns. Ray said he wept while attaching the beads; each one was like a treasured memory of my dad. The sculpture was a gift of inex-pressible love. I believe the joy Ray experienced in giving it was equal to the joy my mom felt in receiv-ing it. Like grace, this gift of selfless love healed a tiny part of Ray's heart in the making of it, and I know it comforts my mom's broken heart whenever she looks at it.

The great American painter, Andrew Wyeth,

said,

I think one's art goes as far and as deep as one's love goes … If I have anything to offer, it is my emotional contact with the place where I live and the people I paint.

When we follow not only our joy but also our sorrow where it leads us, we find that our gifts will serve us and others there, too. In fact, it's especially because it is *our* own unique sorrow that it compels us to respond in ways that are distinctly ours. When we write, dance, sing, or create in other ways to comfort and heal ourselves, often others who are hurting receive from it what they need as well. To creatively work in those places where your skills and compassion intersect with a particular need is to be, in a very real sense, the hands and feet of God in that situation.

Until My Heart Breaks

Take the looking glass away
Put a window in its place
Tired of living like it's all about me
Playing careful staying safe
My heart feels like a cage
I've forgotten what it was to be free
Love invade me
Overtake me
How long will it take

How long will it take
Until my heart breaks
Can't stay the way I was
Can't live unless I love
Wide open without walls, without fear
I surrender I give up
I've been hiding long enough
Wash over me 'til I disappear
Love come break me
Recreate me
How long will it take
How long will it take
Until my heart breaks

("Until My Heart Breaks" by Staci Frenes, Nate Sabin, Adam Moritz ©2012 Stone's Throw Music/ASCAP lorilu music/ASCAP apt 4 publishing/ASCAP)

turning outward

There is nothing more truly artistic
than to love people.
– Vincent van Gogh (painter)

MY FRIEND AND FELLOW SONGWRITER Jason Gray and I were having a conversation recently about—of all things—what it's like to have kids who are following the same creative paths we are. He's got a son and I've got a daughter (Abby) that will likely be pursuing a career in music. Songwriting, arranging, performing—both of our kids have seen us engaging in various aspects of our creative lives over the years and they're starting to experience it themselves and develop a taste for it. We talked about the raw, passionate excitement that seems to gush so freely and unrestrained when we're first discovering what we're good at. Both of our kids are at that stage—it's a blast watching them grow and experiment with their talents right now. Writing a new song, playing on stage, getting better at their instrument. It's all *fun* for them—a creative adrenaline rush—and as parents we're thrilled to see they're pursuing the creative fire in their belly.

But Jason and I agreed that there's a gap between the hot-burning fire of early passion for our gift and the slow disciplined burn of serving others with it. Early in our friendship Jason and I were both independent artists with no record label or radio airplay to speak of, doing our own booking and managing and promoting. It's a lot of hard work with not a lot of acclaim or outward signs of "success". When Jason got a major label record deal a few years ago, we rejoiced—now he didn't have to work so hard (we thought)! Now, all that business stuff would be taken care of for him (we thought)! Now, he could focus on just songwriting (we thought)!

But as we've stayed close friends over the years and shared the ups and downs of our respective careers, I've seen how we've both had to sacrifice some of our idealism and passion on the altar of realistic, practical considerations. Putting in long hours at things we'd rather *not* do in order to keep doing the thing we *do* want to do. The adrenaline rush our kids are experiencing now faded for us a long time ago, and something more deeply rooted and essential grew in its place.

Maturity, selflessness, persistence. These are the sustaining characteristics of a disciplined creative life. It's a paradigm shift we make from *what can my gift do for me?* to *what can my gift do for others?* Creative people are notoriously turned inward: reflecting, ruminating, idea-gathering, and pondering our next work of art, or worse, comparing ourselves with other artists who are more successful and doing better than we are. For the most part, we have a hard time getting out of our own heads. And that self-absorbed stance is where some creative people stay for far too long. But at some point a creative life has to admit that it has fed itself long enough on ambition, money or accolades and is ready to turn outward, see the needs of others and ask the question: *how can I use what I have to help others?* Egos at the door, sleeves up, we hold our talents no longer as badges of merit but as tools of mercy, compassion, justice, love.

As creators in any field, and as believers and followers of Christ, it's crucial that we're constantly checking the alignment of our hearts against what it means to *act justly, love mercy,* and *walk humbly.* This, according to the prophet Micah (6:8), is what God says is *good.* God creates the heaven and earth and all it contains and calls it *good.* Our creativity is *good* when it's lived out in ways that are just, merciful and humble. When we are moved to action by compassion for someone else, we are acting justly, mercifully. Living and creating from a compassionate heart means opening myself fully to another's pain, despair, or hopelessness and offering my gifts to help ease the suffering. To *act* justly in the areas where we're gifted is to move from complacency to creativity.

Two young women I know from Orange County, Los Angeles were moved to action by the injustices they witnessed against young girls kidnapped into India's sex traffic industry. They discovered in their visits with some of these girls that rescuing them from brothels was just the beginning; the girls needed sustainable income in order to provide for themselves and avoid the terrifying but often inevitable pull back into the sex trade. These two women from The OC knew something about fashion, marketing, and fund-raising among LA's rich and famous. They organized benefit events of all kinds to raise awareness for the need, and with the donated funds were able to purchase a warehouse in India, equip it with several sewing machines and begin hiring former prostitutes to create a line of clothing called <u>Punjammies</u>.

As I type this paragraph, I am wearing a pair of Punjammies! They're like pajama bottoms only cuter, and they're available in various lengths and all sorts of gorgeous bright prints. The non-profit organization formed by the two LA friends is called The International Princess Project, and it's been steadily growing over the last few years, adding new items to the clothing line and even purchasing an additional warehouse and storage facility in India. IPP is one of my favorites to follow and support. Their work beautifully illustrates what the power of applied creativity can do to effect change in one specific area of injustice.

Jason and I actually met years ago through another international relief and development organization focusing on the needs of children—World Vision. My sister, the video producer, had been doing some work for them, traveling and producing promotional videos and through her work I saw little glimpses of what World Vision was doing for children. I decided to sponsor a child from Bangladesh, who was my daughter's age at the time, and was amazed at the scope of practical resources World Vision was providing in his village.

I never imagined that my work—writing and singing songs—could intersect with the life-changing work World Vision was doing, but soon after sponsoring, I joined their Artist Associates program alongside other musicians, authors, and actors. This partnership would involve telling people about child sponsorship whenever I was able to do so in the venues where I was singing. The first time I shared about World Vision during one of my concerts I felt an almost tangible light bulb switch on somewhere inside of my soul. I felt flooded with a whole new awareness for the responsibility and honor that comes with having a gift and a platform from which to share it. I realized—and am still realizing—that my gift is not just mine to use for my own advancement, or pleasure, though those things may come. In my case, I've seen the impact that telling stories of others' suffering can have, both in my music and in the words I speak to the audiences that come to hear me.

One of my favorite stories involves a group of us visiting a tiny rural village several miles outside the city of Managua, Nicaragua where World Vision had been working. We'd driven for several hours before coming to a clearing in a grove of trees where we were met by about a dozen kids wearing huge smiles and gleaming identical brand new glasses. The families in this remote village hardly looked like they could afford medical care, much less glasses. I was curious and excited to hear their stories. As someone who suffered from strabismus as a baby, and has a daughter born with the same stigmatism, I know how precious one's eyesight is. I had two corrective eye surgeries as a child; my daughter Abby had the same surgery at age five months and again at two years old. We both had to wear glasses for a while, and without access to health care neither of us would have functioning vision today.

You can imagine how my heart melted seeing these little faces in their new specs. In my broken Spanish, I asked a little group of three girls about their new glasses. The girls excitedly talked over each other, telling me that they'd only been wearing them for a few months, and couldn't believe what a difference it had made—they could see better to do their schoolwork, draw pictures, help their mom with sewing—everything was so much easier now that they could see well. I had to wrangle a translator over to get the full gist of their stories. I tried to convey how excited I was for them, and told them that I, too, wore glasses and had a daughter who had also worn them. I'll never forget the grinning and hand-holding and giggles we shared. I wanted to scoop all three of them up and carry them home in my suitcase.

On the plane ride back to San Francisco I couldn't help comparing these little girls with my own healthy, bright daughter, Abby, waiting for me at home. So alike in all the ways that mattered: what they feared, what they dreamed for their futures, what made them hopeful and what made them sad. And yet so very different in the opportunities available to them simply because of where they were born. It didn't seem fair that Abby should have so much and these three had so little. The eye care and surgery my daughter received were things I'd taken for granted—like a million other resources she'd have access to that these Nicaraguan girls would not.

Telling the stories of children like these is the very least Jason and I can do to help raise awareness and support for the work World Vision is doing, but it is something we can do in the stewardship of the gifts God's given us. It's a small piece in the puzzle of how to "fix" the cycle of poverty, but the ripple effect is surprisingly impactful. For example, I learned that one donor will typically give $3000 over the life of their child sponsorship. For every 1000 kids sponsored at our concerts, $3,000,000 has been given to the poorest of the poor.

The work is much bigger than us, but it's not our work alone. It's inspired by God's heart for the poor, so there is a kind of effortless yoking of our gifts to His will, like two oxen together working a strip of field. We're doing what we've always done, sharing our songs with anyone who wants to listen, and God's doing what He does, loving *the least of these* and stirring hearts to action on their behalf.

Our creative life takes a different shape when it turns outward. It expands, reaching beyond the borders of our own ego and agenda. Serving others with our gifts, in whatever capacity that's best suited to our skills and temperament is an investment in the eternal. Once we begin to see past our own need for awards and accomplishments, we can find a much deeper joy in knowing our gifts are doing a work that will outlive us in ways we could never predict or imagine.

losing and finding

If you lose yourself in your work,
you find who you are.
– Frederick Buechner (author, minister)

MY DEAR FRIENDS NATE AND Lori Sabin first found their way into my heart several years ago when I met Nate through a mutual friend. We began writing songs and then eventually making records together. The Sabins are a creative Power Couple: Lori's a published fiction writer and a talented singer/songwriter who also makes jewelry, mixed media art and plays a mean B-3 organ. Nate's a songwriter, Grammy-nominated record producer, session acoustic guitar player and highly respected choir director and worship leader. They both just ooze talent, and are the sweetest people you'll ever meet. I'm a lifer fan and friend of both.

Over the years I've known and worked with Nate I've seen him consistently choose projects close to his heart, sometimes even at the cost of more high profile work. Understand, Nate is someone with rock-star level talent as a producer, songwriter and musician. Anyone who plays music with Nate experiences his musical brilliance and recognizes that it goes beyond skill to something closer to genius. A fellow artist who's worked with Nate summed it up: "He just *gets* music on a level deeper than anyone else I know." He's written songs and produced for some of the top artists in the Gospel/CCM industry. Nate's talent opens doors and he's walked through many that have earned him mad respect and notoriety. But I've never seen those things become the prime motivating factors for choosing projects—he follows his heart.

One place I've seen Nate invest his heart and passion for as long as I've known him is with the youth choir at his church in St. Paul, MN. Some are the kids from within the congregation, but many come from rough backgrounds and have never stepped foot in a church, much less sung in a church choir. Year after year, as the roster ebbs and flows, Nate works with these kids; rehearsing weekly with the singers and band members, regularly writing new material and charting out the various parts for them to learn. Lori and Nate open their home for choir BBQs and bonfires and jam nights. These kids learn how to read music, play in a band, sing harmony, and most importantly *worship together* as one voice, one team. The Sabins have taken the choir on several cross-country tours—I've seen them perform and they're always energetic and musically off-the-charts good.

I have no idea how many kids have come through Nate's youth choir over the years, but I know several personally who are now full-time artists, songwriters, worship leaders and session musicians. I'm sure Nate and Lori could tell stories of dozens more who've gone on to pursue music in some form or another as adults. But even if they haven't made a career out of music, I can't help but think that the time these kids spend being a part of something so special is pivotal and has a lasting impact. For many, it changes how they see themselves and what they can accomplish with practice, focus, and determination. For others, unexpected lifelong friendships form and become part of the tapestry of their lives forever. It's a rich legacy.

Nate will never know the full ripple-effect his life's work will have on the kids who sing in his youth choirs year after year. There's no way to keep track of all the tangible and intangible ways people are changed by the time and love and talents we invest in them. But we *can* make the decision to pour ourselves into others — in big and small ways — with the confidence that it's worth the cost. And there will be a cost. In Nate's case the accumulated hours he's spent rehearsing and working on charts and arrangements, tours and performances for the youth choir might have been spent on his own music, or producing records for high-paying clients. But I know Nate understands the value of a different kind of payoff, and that's why he continues to sow his love and musical gifts into that particular field. As a result, what continues to grow are kids whose lives will never be the same.

Author Madeleine L'Engle in her book *Walking on Water,* says the mark of a good work of art is the anonymity that happens both on the part of the one who created it, and those who experience it. While she is creating, the artist can often forget herself, because she's listening so intently to the Spirit's inspiration and paying attention to what she's hearing, trying to follow it closely. The sense of self — the ego — is overshadowed by the focus on the work itself. And when we, the "audience", experience what that artist makes, in whatever form it comes to us, we also lose ourselves momentarily in the beauty and imagination it evokes in us. Art — making and receiving it — is transcendent in that way; we become part of something bigger than us in the process.

In this way I think our creative lives echo our spiritual lives. Jesus tells us that whoever saves his life will lose it, and whoever loses his life for His sake will find it. (Matthew 10:39) Our old friend, the servant in the Parable of the Talents who buries what he's given, plays out this truth in unmistakable starkness. It's as though by hiding his talent he's trying desperately to *save himself* from those who might take from him. It's easy to become stingy with our gifts. To pick and choose how we use them based on how high the return will be. To keep them hidden when we suspect we'll be required to sacrifice for those who can do nothing for us. And yet Jesus says we find our lives when we lose them for His sake—which I imagine involves letting go of our agenda and expectations for our talents and offering them to others. Remember, the rewards for investing in God's work is that we then experience the joy of seeing our gifts from an eternal, kingdom perspective. Nothing else even comes close to that joy.

There was a woman who attended the same church I did several years ago (I'll call her Charlene), who had a pretty rough life. She had two kids and was married to a man who was physically and emotionally abusive, although few of us knew the true extent of her suffering. Charlene attended a weekly prayer group at my mom's house once a week, and began to feel safe enough there to tell the ladies about the difficulties with her husband, one of the biggest of which involved her weight. She was obese—at least 100 pounds overweight—and her husband constantly berated her about it. There were other things, too. Her oldest boy was away at college but her youngest son (about 12 at the time) had begun treating her with the same kind of disdain and disrespect that her husband did. She felt trapped in an abusive prison, and in the way people often do when they're told something continuously for so many years, she thought she deserved it and would never know anything better.

One night Charlene got into her car and started driving through the steep and windy Oakland Hills around where she lived. In a letter she wrote me months later, she said that when she got into the car, she had every intention of ending her life by driving off one of the sections of road that extended over the cliffs. But about a month earlier Charlene had bought one of my CDs, which stayed in her car stereo 24/7. It had begun playing that night when she started the ignition. She didn't have the heart to turn it off, so she let it play over and over while she sobbed and tried to find a spot to drive her car over the edge. But she never found it. Charlene said that hearing my voice singing those songs in her car over and over kept her from killing herself that night; her letter said simply, *your music saved my life.*

When I'm feeling discouraged about how my career is progressing, or wonder whether the work I'm doing has any impact, I compare this story of Charlene with the one about the Bargain Bin Guy who told me he bought my CD for a buck. I think about the relative "worth" my music had in both of their lives. And the truth is, I had nothing to do with either outcome. I never know where my songs will go when I breathe myself into them, shape them with imperfect hands and release them with a trembling heart into the world. They may end up in the bargain bin, picked up by disinterested hands. They may end up in the CD player of a lost soul, desperate for the assurance of hope. My responsibility is to simply continue sowing myself and my talents into the opportunities I'm given.

Pouring out our talents in service to others — like I've seen my friend Nate and others do — requires sacrifice, and, sometimes, the simple faith to let go of the work and let it become what God wants it to be. Losing ourselves is a refining process that happens over time with the constant push and pull of our will, ego and ambition against what God's love asks of us. We are transformed in this refining process; we lose our limited view and find an enduring eternal perspective. I wrote about this in the song, "Into the Flame" for my *Meteor Shower* album, which my friend Nate produced.

Into the Flame

Your radiant energy is pulling me
Toward such brilliance I can't breathe
I back away into the dark
And then return
Fly into the flame
One with the fire
No other way

To be consumed
To be sustained
To be changed to be yours
I have to fly into the flame
How is it possible I lose myself
And find a me that is more luminous
Awake alive
Your light and life inside of me
Fly into the flame
One with the fire
No other way
To be consumed
To be sustained
To be changed to be yours
I have to fly into the flame

("Into the Flame" by Staci Frenes, George Cochinni ©2007
Stone's Throw Music/ASCAP Top Boost Music/BMI)

only love lives on

We'll grow in our lives
what we plant with our love.
– Bob Goff (author)

MY COUSIN JAY LOST HIS 16 year-old son Jakob in an unexpected tragic accident a few years ago. The kind of accident that I can only imagine has haunted and tormented Jay and his wife every day since. In their grief, and early on after his death, they planted a cherry tree in their front yard in his memory. They planted it the same month of his death—July—and watched as it grew and began yielding buckets of ripe red cherries the anniversary week of Jakob's death each year. More cherries than they know what to do with. The cherries, Jay tells me, are edible but bitter. Every year as they pick these bitter cherries Jay remembers his beautiful son's sixteen years with them, and the ways he touched them with his kindness, his wisdom, and his love. He sent me pictures this past July of Jakob's Tree, they call it, heavy with plump ripe cherries, and at the end of the email Jay wrote, "Life is bittersweet. We all lose ones we love, but we retain the love they leave with us forever."

I learned that firsthand when my dad passed away from cancer last year. The grief was nearly unbearable for our family. We're very close; my kids grew up having their Papa as a regular fixture in their lives. A loving, kind, patient voice in the midst of any storm—that was my dad. His wisdom and gentle temperament were mainstays throughout my childhood. He was the best listener I knew. Dad added beauty to our lives in many ways. He was a skilled photographer—his photos were works of art, and more than a few are matted and framed on our walls. He also drew, painted, and even sculpted a bit in his earlier days. He was skilled at woodworking, too: he built decks, cabinets, potting benches, tables and quirky garden pieces. He loved visiting the seasonal art exhibits at the Palace of Fine Arts or Legion of Honor Art Museum in San Francisco, and was never without his camera when we headed for the beach.

I miss not only him, but also the things he loved that I experienced because he was in my life. I can't imagine a world without all the beauty he pointed out in it. I had a conversation with a close friend of mine during those early tender months when I was in such despair over losing him. My friend wisely said to me, "He's not gone. He's still with you in the different ways you see him in each other." He was so right. My dad *is* with us still. The keen sense of composition and lighting so striking in his photography live on in my sister, a successful film and video producer and editor. Our daughter Abby also has her Papa's sharp eye for photography and art; my brother shares an appreciation for great books and movies with my dad. Our niece, Gabby, sketches beautifully, reminding me of my dad's old charcoal and pencil sketchbooks full of intricately drawn hands and faces and Escher-like staircases. Our son, Zach, has my dad's patient, calm temperament.

I, of course, got my dad's love of music. Although he couldn't carry a tune too far, Dad was an active listener and appreciated great music. When I was a little girl we used to listen to records together, lying on our backs in the living room after dinner. We'd listen in the dark, side-by-side, trying to pick out the different instruments in the arrangements—like trying to find a thimble in one of those *I, Spy* pictures. We'd laugh at each other's guesses sometimes, and I think he purposely called instruments out of left field just to make me giggle, like "banjo!" in a classical piece.

I felt something magical happen in those sessions. I dreamed, and let my mind explore worlds the music created in my imagination. It felt like time out of time—a chance to experience something extraordinary. I'm sure there were a hundred other things my dad could have been doing, but by spend-

ing time with me sharing something we both loved,
he passed along not only his appreciation for music,
but also his curiosity and imagination. He was a student of the universe, and was never too busy to
wonder and enjoy its mysteries.

When Dad was diagnosed with cancer, I decided
to write him a few poems and read them to him as
they came to me—nothing fancy, just memories that
expressed how much I loved him. This one's about
us listening to music together.

Remember the time
we lay on the floor
with the lights out
in front of the stereo console
in the living room
listening to
"Jesus Christ, Superstar"?
Staring up at the ceiling,
we were in our own private
symphony hall.
Song after song we listened
and tried to make out
the different instruments we heard.
Is that a French horn?
I think it's an oboe.
Speaking in hushed, reverent tones
so as not to disrupt the beauty
that enveloped us
I learned to hear music

in parts and counterparts,
in the almost silence and
in the crashing crescendos.
In the resonance and the dissonance,
As I am slowly learning to hear
The voice of God

I feel my dad's love for us, and his love for the beauty around him in what he left with us and in us. Like Nana and the clothes she made, he lives on tangibly in the many photographs and art pieces he left us, and intangibly in the memories we carry and pass on to one another. The things we spent time doing together—the trips to the beach, the art museums, the meals around his table sharing thoughts, opinions, dreams—those are the seeds he planted. I find flowers blooming in my life over and over from those seeds. I find them in the ways I pay attention to beauty like he did; in the things I value, like time with my family, the way he did. So many of the things he loved live on in me.

I was walking every day during the last few months of my dad's life past <u>the garden near my house</u> I wrote about early on in this book. I watched that little garden grow along with the father and his children, knowing that what it yielded would not only be actual vegetables but also the fruit of their time spent together. Love, laughter, companionship, trust—a harvest that his children would reap in the years to come. I saw this as I knew my own father only had weeks left to live, and I knew that even in his dying there would be life. His love was a generative force; what he sowed into us still grows and blooms in his wake.

Any gardener will tell you there's a necessary cycle that happens in the growth of a healthy plant. Jesus talks about this cycle as a metaphor for the death and resurrection necessary for new life within each of us. *Unless a grain of wheat falls into the earth and dies, it remains alone; but if it dies, it bears much fruit.* (John 12:24) It's hard to imagine our lives beyond the years we have breath and blood still flowing through us, but if we could see that the people and things we invest ourselves in, consistently and over time, can and will outlive us, would we live differently? Is it possible to create and do meaningful, beautiful work with our eyes fixed beyond the borders of our ego, our agenda, our need for affirmation and fame? If it is, we have to think like a gardener. We have to understand the cycle of death and rebirth as it relates to our own deepest desires.

Who would have known all those years ago that returning home from Nashville with no record deal was just one of the many deaths I would experience in my creative life in order for it to grow into what it was meant to be? That discouraging December night when I started this book was another. It's the essential cycle. We pour ourselves into the fields in front of us, to those places our joy and our sorrow take us, with the abandon and joy of a child, letting go of our expectations, agendas, and hopes for what the work might become. Only then can we can fully release it for what it was intended to do.

What grows where we've sown our gifts may surprise us, because it's both a part of us and *other* than us. It has our imprint, our stamp, our distinct personality; but like the songs I write, or the clothes Nana sewed, the books my author friends publish, or the watercolors my artist friends paint, our creative work becomes something else when experienced by others. We hope it will have meaning, we hope it will connect, we hope it will communicate what we love in a way that is equal to the vision we have for it. But ultimately we can only do our part in offering who we are and what we have to give.

I challenge you to cultivate your own creative life; one that recognizes your unique offering to the people God places in your path. Listen to your life—what you love and what breaks your heart, and work through the resistance that keeps you from the work that's closest to those things. Stay connected to the Holy Spirit, paying attention to His life inside of you and the world around you, living in community, working together. And most of all, be confident that the sowing of your precious self—your time, energy, talents and love—will grow a garden of abundant fruit that will live beyond the boundaries of your finite years.

Only Love Lives On

Open up your hands
Take what the giver has for you
To harvest and to plant
Faithful in the work he's called you to
Pray for something good to grow
When it comes to you you'll know
All we have is here and gone
When the day is done
Only love lives on
Open up your eyes
See a field of beauty in your wake
On and on through time
Every note of love resonates
The song you sing has always been
Add your voice but in the end
All we have is here and gone
Fading like the setting sun
All we leave is all we've loved
When the day is done
Only love lives on

("Only Love Lives On" by Staci Frenes, Nate Sabin ©2012 Stone's
Throw Music/ASCAP; Lorilu music/ASCAP)

creative action: Sow and Reap

Reader Reflection Questions

Is there a looming project you'd like to complete? Name the noun — the end result. Then work from the end backwards to the place where you need to start, or restart. Create a set of small, daily or weekly do-able steps that connect the start point to the end result. Commit.

The story of Lilith and the quilt is a powerful example for me of how we can love someone in a tangible way with our talents. List one (or some) specific instance(s) where you were able to bring someone joy, comfort or hope with your creativity.

Compare the experience above with those times you've felt undervalued, demeaned, unappreciated in your creative life. What made the two experiences so different?

Our empathy for others often defines and guides our creative lives. Think about specific groups, or people you long to reach out to and help. Where could you offer your time or talents in order to provide healing, dignity or some other form of help to these people or groups?

Have there been times when you've been tempted to hide or downplay your talent or strengths? For example, when you thought it might require personal sacrifice of you, or when you knew there wouldn't be a 'high return' on your time and effort. Think about why you did or didn't give yourself fully to that situation.

What aspects of your own agenda or ego are attached to the creative work you do? Think about what you're holding on to, and what it might take for you to 'die' as Jesus talks about in John 12:24, in order for your work to fully live.

In what ways have you communicated the things you love through your creativity?

Think about the people and opportunities God has placed in your path – your job, your family, close friends, faith community and co-workers. Now consider the seeds he's placed in your hands – your particular gifts, talents and personality traits. Only you know the full extent to which you've 'sown yourself' into your fields. What do you think grows there as a result of the time, talents and energy you've invested?

notes

Introduction

"Throw Yourself Like Seed" by Miguel De Unamuno from
Poems to Live By In Uncertain Times. Murray, John, Editor.
Boston; Beacon Press, 2002. Print.

Frenes, Staci. Music Page
http://stacifrenes.bandcamp.com/music

Nana and Me

"Letter to Artists" by Pope John Paul II. 1999.
www.vatican.va/holy_father/john_paul_ii/letters/documents/
hf_jp-ii_let_23041999_artists_en.html Web.

Calling it Good

Houseden, Roger.
http://www.amazon.com/Roger-Housden/e/B001IGODW6

L'Engle, Madeline. *Walking on Water*. Northpoint Press,
1995. Print.

Dillard, Annie. Life Magazine *The Big Picture* 1988. Interview.

Parvis, Sara. *Irenaeus: Life Scripture, Legacy* Fortress Press,
2012. Print.

Frenes, Staci. *Breathless* from *Everything You Love Comes Alive* Stone's Throw Music/ASCAP, 2012. Song. http://stacifrenes.bandcamp.com/track/breathless
`

Frenes, Staci. *Picasso's Blues* from *Mosaic* Stone's Throw Music/ASCAP, 2007. Song.

Talents, Big and Small

Frenes, Staci and Sabin, Nate. *Only Love Lives On* from *Everything You love Comes Alive* Stone's Throw Music/lorilu music/ASCAP, 2012. Song. http://stacifrenes.bandcamp.com/track/only-love-lives-on

Children at Play

Gaman, Neil. *The Ocean at the End of the Lane* William Morrow Books, 2013. Print.

Frenes, Staci. *Wise Men and Angels* Stone's Throw Music/ASCAP, 2008. CD http://stacifrenes.bandcamp.com/album/wise-men-and-angels

Remember What We Forgot

Picasso, Pablo. Various Quotations. http://www.quotationspage.com/quotes/Pablo_Picasso/ Web.

Bayles, David and Orland, Ted. *Art and Fear* Image Continuum Press, 2001. Print.

Hemingway, Ernest (quote) from Thorpe, Twyla. *The Crea-*

tive Habit New York, Simon and Schuster, 2003. Print.

Frenes, Staci and Sabin, Nate. *I Suppose* from *Meteor Shower* Stone's Throw Music, lorilu music/ASCAP,2008. Song. http://stacifrenes.bandcamp.com/track/i-suppose

Andrews, Al. http://itsalandrews.com/speaking/ Website.

The Full Measure of You

Frenes, Staci and Chen, Kenon. *Right Now* from *Nothing Short of Amazing Stone's Throw Music,* Flavor 18 Music/ASCAP, 2006.
http://stacifrenes.bandcamp.com/track/right-now Song.

Worth More

Macleod, Hugh from http://gapingvoid.com/ Web.

Frenes, Staci. *Nobody Loves Me Like You* from *Everything You Love Comes Alive* Stone's Throw Music, 2012. Song. stacifrenes.bandcamp.com/track/nobody-loves-me-like-you Song.

Fearless

Chilton Pearce, Joseph.
http://en.wikipedia.org/wiki/Joseph_Chilton_Pearce Web.

Pressfield, Steven. *The War of Art* Black Irish Entertainment, 2012. Print.

Frenes, Staci *The Thief and the Lover* from *Everything You*

Love Comes Alive Stone's Throw Music, 2012.
http://stacifrenes.bandcamp.com/track/the-thief-and-the-lover
Song.

Breathe In

O'Connor, Flannery *A Prayer Journal.* Farr, Strauss and Giroux, 2013. Print.

St. Paul's Cathedral, The Whispering Gallery.
www.atlasobscura.com/places/whispering-gallery-at-st-paul-s-cathedral Web.

Glibert, Elizabeth "Your Elusive Creative Genius" TED Talk http://www.ted.com/talks/elizabeth_gilbert_on_genius Web

Frost, Robert.
http://en.wikiquote.org/wiki/Robert_Frost Web.

Frenes, Staci and Sabin, Nate *Know Your Voice* from *Meteor Shower* Stone's Throw Music, lorilu music/ASCAP, 2008.
http://stacifrenes.bandcamp.com/track/know-your-voice
Song.

Find Your Flow

Graham, Martha
http://en.wikipedia.org/wiki/Martha_Graham Web.

Cohen, Leonard "Zen and the Art of Songwriting" from Fresh Air WHYY on NPR.
www.npr.org/templates/story/story.php?storyId=102692227

Web Interview.

"Dreaming Us" World Vision video
http://www.youtube.com/watch?v=VKb7yBxHXuY

Produced by Heidi Groff at Cinemation Media
http://www.cinemationmedia.com/. Web/Video.

Do What You Love

Barks, Coleman. *The Essential Rumi.* Harper One, 2004.
Print.

Shaw, Luci. *Breath for the Bones* Thomas Nelson, 2009.
Print.

Schultz, Alison. Material Impressions, LLC.
http://www.mypillowsandquilts.com/quilts/ Website.

Rubin, Gretchen. *The Happiness Project.* Harper, 2011. Print.

Frenes, Staci *Everything You Love Comes Alive* from *Everything You Love Comes Alive* Stone's Throw Music, 2012.
https://stacifrenes.bandcamp.com/track/everything-you-love-comes-alive Song.

Pay Attention

Pound, Ezra
www.goodreads.com/quotes/76780-glance-is-the-enemy-of-vision Web Quote.

Frenes, Staci and Sabin, Nate. *Meteor Shower* from *Meteor*

Shower Stone's Throw Music, lorilu music/ASCAP, 2008. http://stacifrenes.bandcamp.com/track/meteor-shower Song.

Stranger Than Fiction Directed by Marc Forster, Screenplay by Zach Helm., 2006. Film.

Frenes, Staci. *That's How You Woo Me* from *Everything You Love Comes Alive* Stone's Throw Music, ASCAP,2012. http://stacifrenes.bandcamp.com/track/thats-how-you-woo-me Song.

Focus Your Lens

Einstein, Albert. Official Einstein Website. http://einstein.biz/quotes.php Quote.

Man on Wire. Directed by James Marsh, 2008. Film.

Godin, Seth. *Purple Cow* Portfolio, 2009. Print.

Lori's Jewelry (The Infamous Button Necklace) www.girlymuse.com/wp-content/uploads/2012/01/IMG_7192-768x1024.jpg

Make Mistakes

Gaman, Neil. "Make Good Art" Commencement Address to University of the Arts Graduates, 2012. http://www.uarts.edu/neil-gaiman-keynote-address-2012 Speech.

Glass, Ira. "The Gap" http://vimeo.com/85040589 Video.

Frenes, Abby. "Cat" Mixed Media Collage, 2011
stacifrenes.com/2011/10/work-of-art-seminar-in-la/creative-life-slide-abby-painting/ Photo.

Kent, Corita. Art Rules
https://www.corita.org/education/19-corita-kent-art-rules.html. Web.

Close, Chuck. "Notes to Self" CBS News.
www.cbsnews.com/news/chuck-closes-advice-to-his-younger-self/ Video.

Nothing Is Wasted

Babauta, Leo. Zen Habits with Bernard Haux.
http://zenhabits.net/pixar/ Web Interview.

Kent, Corita. Art Rules
www.corita.org/education/19-corita-kent-art-rules.html. Web.

Bayles, David and Orland, Ted. *Art and Fear* Image Continuum Press, 2001. Print.

Pressfield, Steven. *The War of Art* Black Irish Entertainment, 2012. Print.

Frenes, Staci and Sabin, Nate. *More Like Your Father* from *Everything You Love Comes Alive* Stone's Throw Music, 2012. stacifrenes.bandcamp.com/track/more-like-your-father Song.

Seek Connection

Whitman, Walt. *A Noiseless Patient Spider*. http://www.poetryfoundation.org/poem/174741 Poem.

Play Your Part

U2 *Beautiful Day* www.youtube.com/watch?v=co6WMzDOh1o&feature=kp Video.

Commit

Fujimura, Matkoto. *A Letter To Young Artists* www.makotofujimura.com/writings/a-letter-to-a-young-artist/. Blog Post.

Murray, William Hutchinson. *The Scottish Himalayan Expedition*. J.M. Dent & Sons, 1951. Print.

Frenes, Staci. *The Great Divide* from *Nothing Short of Amazing* Stone's Throw Music/ASCAP, 2004 http://stacifrenes.bandcamp.com/track/the-great-divide Song.

Momentum

Tharp, Twyla. *The Creative Habit* Simon and Schuster, 2006. Print.

Miller, Donald. *A Million Miles in a Thousand Years*. Thomas Nelson, 2009. Print.

Rush, Barbara. *Dark Work* FastPencil, Inc. 2011. Print.
NPR Radio's "Oliver Sacks Observes the Mind Through Music" www.npr.org/2007/11/13/16110162/oliver-sacks-observes-the-mind-through-music Web Interview.

Follow Your (Broken) Heart

Barry, Wendall. *Jayber Crow* Counterpoint, 2001. Print.

Project Linus. http://www.projectlinus.org/ Website.

Buechner, Frederick.
en.wikipedia.org/wiki/Frederick_Buechner. Web.

Ray's Tree http://stacifrenes.com/2014/06/rays-tree/rays-tree-sculpture

Wyeth, Andrew. http://www.andrewwyeth.com/ Website.

Frenes, Staci; Sabin, Nate; Moriz, Adam. *Until My Heart Breaks* from *Everything You Love Comes Alive*. Stone's Throw Music, lorilu music, apt 4 Publishing/ASCAP, 2012. stacifrenes.bandcamp.com/track/until-my-heart-breaks Song.

Turning Outward

VanGogh, Vincent. *Letter to Theo VanGogh*.
http://www.webexhibits.org/vangogh/letter/18/538.htm Web.

Gray, Jason. http://jasongraymusic.com/ Website.

International Princess Project. http://intlprincess.org/ Web-site.

World Vision. http://stacifrenes.com/world-vision/ Artist Associate Website.

Losing and Finding

Buechner, Frederick.
http://en.wikipedia.org/wiki/Frederick_Buechner. Web.

Sabin, Nate. *Chase the Wind* (worship music and resources) natesabin.com/ctw/Catch_the_Wind_Worship/Team.html Website.

L'Engle, Madeline *Walking on Water.* Northpoint Press, 1995. Print.

Frenes, Staci; Cocchini, George. *Into the Flame* from *Meteor Shower.* Stone's Throw Music, Top Boost Music/ASCAP, 2008.   http://stacifrenes.bandcamp.com/track/into-the-flame Song.

Only Love Lives On

Goff, Bob. *Love Does.* Thomas Nelson, 2012. Print.

Photographs by Dad (just a few…)
http://stacifrenes.com/2010/10/a-few-pictures-for-you/

The garden near my house.
stacifrenes.com/2014/04/wildandpreciouslife/only-love-lives-

on-meme/

Frenes, Staci and Sabin, Nate. *Only Love Lives On* from *Everything You Love Comes Alive* Stone's Throw Music, lori-lu music/ASCAP, 2012.
stacifrenes.bandcamp.com/track/only-love-lives-on Song

acknowledgements

THIS BOOK IS A TAPESTRY that's been years in the making and reflects the many threads of love, encouragement and inspiration of some amazing people in my life.

Many thanks to…

Abe, Zachary and Abby, for inspiring me every day, and for putting up with my glassy-eyed, distracted self while writing this book. I love you.

Mom, for reading everything I write and loving it.

Lori Sabin, for lovingly nudging me through this process, and for your mad editing skills in getting the manuscript into shape.

Melissa Riddle-Chalos, for advice and guidance. Your expertise and valuable input arrived at the perfect time.

Mandi Higgins, for reading this in its various stages and encouraging me to keep at it, and for your smart, funny insight.

Philip Nation, for offering wise counsel from the very beginning stages, and for your unwavering belief that I had this book in me.

Jason Gray and Nate Sabin, for the many conversations about art and faith that inspired me to dig deeper while writing this book.

Marci Lapiore, Amy Galbraith, Andrea Eldridge, Phil Aud, Melissa Campbell-Goodson and Scott Riggan, for reading this in the editing stages and providing me with much needed feedback.

Judy Mikalonis, for confirming — professionally and personally — that this message is worth sharing.

Jon at Usborne Artistry, for designing this beautiful cover.

Julie at JT Formatting, for your expertise and top-notch service.

Finally, to the friends and family members who allowed me to include your stories in this book. I know your acts of love and creativity will inspire others as much as they have me.

about the author

STACI FRENES is a singer/songwriter whose folky-pop music has inspired audiences at her concerts all over the country, and aired on major network TV shows such as *The Biggest Loser, America's Next Top Model,* and *All My Children.* Staci is also a World Vision artist associate, and has recently added author and conference speaker to her resume. She and her husband, Abe, have two children and live near San Francisco, California where she enjoys the breathtaking scenery, fabulous wine and robust coffee.

Visit Staci at http://www.stacifrenes.com

Stay connected with Staci on Facebook at
http://www.facebook.com/stacifrenes

16278194R00122

Made in the USA
San Bernardino, CA
26 October 2014